26 Years to Eternity

Lizzie White

Onwards and Upwards Publishers
3 Radfords Turf, Cranbrook, Exeter,
EX5 7DX, United Kingdom.
www.onwardsandupwards.org

This first edition published in the United Kingdom by Onwards and Upwards Publishers (2018).

ISBN: 978-1-78815-627-1
Typeface: Sabon LT
Graphic design: LM Graphic Design

Printed in the United Kingdom.

Endorsements

This is a wonderful and inspiring read, illustrating the personal journey of a grieving mother over the loss of her deeply loved son, Robbie, who was tragically and suddenly killed in an accident. From the very first chapter to the last, her story evoked in me tears, laughter and many other emotions. It is an easy book to read in one sitting. Lizzie shares with us the importance for her in having the space to grieve, yet at the same time longing for the recognition by others that the impact of grief can last for years. The anguish she shares and her struggles as a Christian in trying to make sense of suffering from a biblical point of view are very profound. But this is not only a story about Lizzie. She also paints a wonderful, colourful picture of Robbie, a one-in-a-million young man – kind-hearted, easy going and full of fun – who touched the lives of many in different ways. He lived life to the full and with a Christian faith, was not afraid to die. Robbie is a unique and unforgettable character who will continue to live on in the memory of many. This is an unforgettable story which I encourage you to read. I am sure it will touch your heart like it did mine.

Christine Ledger
Author, Counsellor, Tutor

Christine Ledger has worked for many years as a counsellor. She is a regular tutor on CWR's courses and has co-authored many of their Insight books on subjects such as low self-esteem, anxiety, depression, anger, assertiveness, perfectionism and conflict.

As someone who lost a brother in a car accident, the feelings described in this book are only too familiar. As a Christian, I can relate to wrestling with the tough questions of faith. In this refreshingly honest account, Lizzie describes how she's found glimmers of hope in the midst of despair and doubt. This book can give the grieving some reassurance that the feelings they are experiencing are 'normal' and give those supporting them a valuable insight into the difficult journey.

Nicki Wisdom
Brothers and Sisters: Life after loss, Care for the Family

About the Author

Lizzie White graduated with a First-Class degree in Psychology in 1991 from the University of Reading. Thereafter she worked for eighteen years in the School of Psychology and Clinical Language Sciences on numerous externally-funded psychology research projects. Lizzie is currently part of the executive support team within the School supporting academic research.

Lizzie and her husband Nigel enjoy spending time with their grown-up children, walking in the countryside, being creative and tending their garden. Lizzie also plays the violin and mandolin and has played in local string orchestras. A churchgoer all her life, Lizzie and Nigel are active members of Greyfriars Church in the centre of Reading.

Twenty-Six Years to Eternity was written after one day changed life forever when Lizzie's twenty-six-year-old son Robbie was tragically killed in an accident on his journey to work. The last three years have been a test of Lizzie's faith in God, a journey searching for answers, a longing to come to a place of comparative peace.

This book is dedicated with deep gratitude and love:

To my husband, my beloved Nigey,
who daily walks this difficult road with me.

And to my children:
To my precious sons, Robbie and Jack,
united in God's love;
I am so blessed to be your mum.
To my lovely daughters, Tabby and Millie;
I am so privileged to be your second mum.

With love and thanks too:

To my dear family,
especially Dad, Mum, Ali, Netta, Harriet, Ben, Mike.
To our friends, Robbie's friends and the church community,
To Kelly and Dick.
And to the counsellors who have helped us all.

Contents

Prologue

ITV NEWS, MERIDIAN
13th June, 12.40pm.

Thames Valley Police is appealing for information following a fatal collision in Finchampstead this morning.

Thames Valley Police is appealing for information after a motorcyclist was killed in a collision in Finchampstead. Police were called by the ambulance service at 6.39am to reports of a collision between a silver Nissan Note and a black Yamaha motorcycle on the A327. The driver of the Nissan, a 33-year-old man from Hampshire, was arrested on suspicion of causing death by dangerous driving. He remains in police custody. The road remains closed in both directions while collision investigators examine the scene. Motorists are advised to avoid the area.[1]

[1] *www.itv.com/news/meridian/story/2014-06-13/fatal-collision-in-finchampstead*

SESSION 1

The Need for Water

This is the most difficult part to tell the counsellor. She is waiting patiently, watching me as I pull out another tissue and wipe my eyes.

'The call came through when we were out walking,' I finally manage to say.

She is still watching me, waiting for me to go on. But how to even form the words? How to give a voice to the horror, the devastation, the sudden piercing pain, the shattering of everything that that moment brought? My own dear precious son, whose life throughout the whole of my adult years has been intertwined with my own... How can my life ever continue without his?

'And?' The counsellor is looking at me gently. 'Tell me about the call.'

I am in Cyprus with Nigey. We have been together for a long time now through all the usual ups and downs of family life plus the extra complications of being a blended family. But now that Millie, the youngest, is almost eighteen, we have escaped for a couple of weeks on our own – to Cyprus, the island where we spent our honeymoon. It is only a few days into the first week when somehow I manage to put my back out – badly. So, we are spending a lot of time trying to walk it off along the beautiful deserted beaches. And this treatment is working. My back is on the mend. Millie rings to say she has passed her driving test. Jack is in Barcelona for a few days enjoying a break after his finals. Tabby is about to start going into the clinics for her chiropractor's final year. And Robbie is on a wind-down: three weeks left of school and then his wedding. After a stormy, cloudy first week, the sun is out and the temperature is "hotting up". We are starting to relax.

It is Friday, June 13th and after the weekend we will be flying home. The maids have been and gone early and we are getting ready to head into the little town for more water. Only when I bend down to get my flip-flops, there is a sudden sharp whipping of pain across my back, clenching me in a gripping spasm, causing me to cry out.

'Looking back now, with the two hours' time difference, that was the same time it happened.'

'So, you went out for more water?'

'Yes. It was about a twenty-minute walk from our villa. But we hadn't gone far...'

As we walk up the hill, past arable land and the farmhouse, Nigey's mobile is ringing. By the time he has retrieved his phone from his pocket, the ringing has stopped.

'Private number,' he tells me. 'Some insurance company, nuisance call probably.'

But almost immediately it is ringing again. This time he answers. I know instantly something is wrong. *Really* wrong. I am standing next to him, not panicking, not anxious. Just nothing. The call is brief. He looks at me, takes my hands and says straight out, 'This is the worse news we could have. The worst news we could *possibly* have. Robbie's been killed in an accident.'

I have said it. I have told the counsellor. I have put those two words together in one sentence; two words that shouldn't ever go together. I am crying, tears pouring down my face. As I recount all this to her, it is as though I am somewhere floating, looking down on myself and Nigey; as though we are just characters in a play, actors in a film. And I think how much better it would be if she asked Nigey about this. All I can do is tell her the facts. There are no words I can give to my feelings, nothing that can convey that moment.

I am sitting in the farmhouse now. But I am still screaming. Screaming and screaming and screaming. I want to tear at myself, rip myself apart, try and let some of the pain out because it is suffocating me, drowning me, consuming me and there is nowhere for the pain to go but inside me. And the pain keeps coming and coming. I want to surrender myself to it, let it destroy me too.

The woman is drenching me, pouring cold water all over my face. But still I am screaming and screaming and screaming.

And now I am with Nigey in a truck and we are being driven by the woman's son to the hospital. But I want to get away; I want to run, I want to escape this pain, this moment, this horror. And I am screaming and screaming and screaming.

'So, the people from the farmhouse you were walking past when the call came through, they took you into their home and tried to help you? And then they took you to the hospital?'

I nod at the counsellor.

Outside the hospital there is another call and this time the policeman wants to talk to me. But nothing is making sense. I keep telling him that I need to know Robbie wasn't alone. I am desperate for him to tell me that Robbie wasn't alone. He *must* tell me that Robbie wasn't alone. But he doesn't tell me that. He is firm and simply deals with facts.

He gives me a time of death. It is too far from the time he tells me that the accident happened. All I think is that it can't be right; Robbie can't have been struggling on his own all that time. I tell the policeman again that Robbie mustn't have been alone, but he doesn't listen to me.

The call has ended.

The counsellor looks at me and glances over to the clock on the table. She is kind and she is trying to help. But I am just another client and in ten minutes my session will be over.

I am in a taxi with Nigey being driven back to the villa. We need to get home, sort out a flight. In the hospital I have spoken to Millie and to Robbie's fiancée, who are with the policeman, and having refused to be sedated, I have been given some Valium. And I have stopped screaming. I am feeling numb, unreal, detached and totally, utterly empty. I feel nothing. It is as though I too have ceased to exist. I have a body but I am not here. It is my body that opens the suitcases and shoves everything in; that rings Mum, who will let Jack know (as he is near them) and the others; that speaks several times to Kelly, the Police Family Liaison Officer and discusses donating Robbie's tissues; that walks again with Nigey into the town as we need money and we still need water; that talks to Jack and to others; that waits the ten long hours before we can get a flight back.

Lizzie has left. The Lizzie that was me has died too.

I know that I am mixing up tenses, that I am jumping about in my story, but I also know enough from my years in psychology that the counsellor will be looking out for 'Unresolved Grief'.

It is almost too much, the standing in the queue out on the tarmac to board the plane. It is dark; it is late now. I am desperate to be home yet I am really struggling to stay in this line, to nudge inch by inch forwards as all the others are doing, to be ready to find my seat when I get on board; all these routine, normal, mundane things that everyone is doing, that I used to do. It is making me anxious, panicked, forming a tight knot in my stomach. I am whimpering, not screaming now, not crying again, yet. My face must be crumpled, distorted, anguished, as the whole of me is. Everyone must know that my entire world has come crashing down, the me of yesterday has been crushed and gone. But no one looks at me. No one sees me. My whole being is shrieking out that I have lost my son, but no one hears me. They file past onto the plane as though nothing is different, nothing has changed. It is almost too much, but this body that seems to keep on working regardless moves my legs forwards and I file on too.

'So, you manage after a very long wait to get on board the plane?' I nod again.

But my seat isn't with Nigey's. He managed to get this flight sorted for us but it is a Friday night in June and a lot of other holidaymakers are flying home. And this now, this is too much for me. I am crying. It isn't the crying that I used to do, it's from deep down, gripping my stomach – wails from a place far inside of me I hadn't known existed.

The lady next to me is unbuckling her seat belt, talking to a man next to Nigey. They are going to swap seats for us. But the stewardess is here too and she is gently helping me up. Nigey is here and we are moving along the aisle to the front where there is a row of empty seats.

'So, you *did* manage to sit together? The stewardess sorted you out a place?'

'Yes, she was very kind. She sat with us for some of the four-hour flight. She was very young but she had lost a friend in similar circumstances a few months ago and she could sympathise with us.'

But it is the moment at the airport, at Gatwick, that is etched most in my mind from all that long journey home...

I am with Nigey pulling our cases through customs and out into the arrivals hall. I am still here standing under the archway, the concourse spread out before me, when I see Jack. He has refused to listen to me; not taken my concerns on board. He has been insistent. Despite his distressed state, he has driven down from Birmingham to Reading and then on, this evening, in a violent thunderstorm, with my dad to Gatwick. Seeing him, my heart breaks. And I crumple. Right there, in everyone's way, I collapse. My body finally succumbs. I am crying, wailing, alien noises throbbing from deep down inside me, gasping for air, drowning, no longer able to go on. But Jack is with me, holding me. His arms, joining with Nigey's and my dad's, enfold me.

The counsellor holds out her tissue box. I take one automatically and wipe my eyes. It is a procedure I have followed countless times now. It is so hard, this going over and over things; so difficult to make myself understood, to get my point across, to find the right words. *Any* words. I want the counsellor to realise just how special Robbie was, Robbie is. Not just to me but to so many people whose lives he touched. And how special he is to God.

I want to convey to her that he was just a normal person, full of life, full of fun, full of mischief. He got some things wrong, he got some things right. He was no saint – how many of us can say that we are? – but one thing that was central to him was his belief in Jesus. I want her to know that God doesn't call perfect people, he calls ordinary people like Robbie, like her, like me.[2]

But I do like talking about my living memories, sharing with the counsellor the remarkable yet humble person that Robbie was, describing to her his humour, his zest for life, his service to others, his love, his faith.

It is vivid red, flaming, nestled in his hand.

He is part turned away from the open doorway as I stand there on the landing, horror gripping me in an instant. The smooth pale skin of his naked bottom, the crumpled heap of trousers wound round his ankles, clothes discarded in a hurry… I feel a lump in my throat. He is my precious three-year-old son, vulnerable, exposed, defenceless – and with a horrendously discoloured willy.

My first thought as I hurl myself into the bathroom to reach him is that he has burnt it. But he is peeing happily, splashing copious amounts of wee around the toilet rather than in the bowl. So, no pain then…

He grins as I risk the unsteady flow of urine and crouch down.

'Oh, my days, Robbie! What on earth has happened? What have you done to your willy?' I shriek.

'What, Mum?'

'Your willy, sweetheart. It looks so red. Is your willy sore?'

'I coloured it in.'

'What? Coloured it in?' I repeat slowly to grasp his meaning. But he has already yanked his trousers up and is about to flush and go and play. 'Hands!' I remind him, turning on the taps for him to dangle them under the flow of water. Then I continue, 'What do you mean, *coloured it in?*'

'With felt tip. At nursery.'

He has always been a couple of steps ahead of me, this son of mine. At three he is performing a student stunt with two of his friends at nursery. I am surprised no one had noticed the three of them, pants and trousers down, busy with their pens…

[2] See 1 Corinthians 1:26-29.

'He sounds like he was a real character – gave you a lot of fun.'
'Gives us a lot of fun,' I correct the counsellor.

I lean over in the pew to catch Robbie's eye as he lies on his bed of kneelers under the pew in front. I can't remember now when he first did this in church, but it has become his little game once he is back in the main church after Sunday School. He crawls out and takes my hand as we both stand up to walk down the aisle for Communion. Robbie is wearing his blue, burgundy-trimmed balaclava. As we approach, he tugs the top down so that his face is completely concealed, and on we go together, me and my four-year-old son looking for all the world like he is ready to rob the nearest bank. And as we kneel side by side at the altar rail, the vicar places his hand on the brightly knitted head and blesses him.

'That must have caused the vicar some amusement,' the counsellor notes, smiling at me.

Robbie is in Year 6 at school and I am in church again, sitting crammed into a pew with hundreds of other parents, grandparents, uncles, aunts, siblings, friends. Nativity time. Robbie is a silver angel. His teacher has enlisted the boys to be angels, gold, silver and bronze. They are wearing white gowns. I only know this because Robbie has told me. I haven't slaved away at the sewing machine as the other mums have.

'An angel! What about your costume?' My heart plummets thinking I will have to heave the old sewing machine in from the garage and spend a few wretched evenings in front of it.

'All done! Well, apart from bringing in some tinsel.'

'But what are you going to wear?'

'Oh, just this white gown thingy. Don't worry, Mum. I was meant to bring the material home for you to sew like all the others have, but I said to Mrs Woolett that my Mum can't sew – so she's doing it.'

I sit in the pew, still a little embarrassed, but that has mostly been replaced by thankfulness that Robbie's outfit will now definitely not fall apart on stage.

‘We had an email recently from Robbie’s Year 6 teacher,’ I tell the counsellor now. ‘She was remembering about that angel costume; thinking back to when he was in church having fun with the other angels. He is with the angels right now. But it is too soon for him to be there, surely? Surely twenty-six is too soon?’

'Bye, Robbie!'

The door shuts behind him. I go back into the kitchen to finish clearing up and almost immediately the doorbell rings.

Someone is charging down the stairs. 'It's only Robbie.'

'What have you forgotten?' I ask.

'Jus' my keys, thanks. On the stairs.'

The door shuts again and this time he is off.

Session 2

Custard for Breakfast

The counsellor has asked me to bring in some photos to show her some pictures of Robbie, share with her some of my stories.

'Here he is aged about seventeen or eighteen,' I say, passing the counsellor a very happy picture of Robbie with long hair tied back, full beard.

'What a handsome chap!' she exclaims.

'Actually, that must have been when he was in Year 13, so he would've been eighteen. About the time of his A levels. There's a funny story about his maths exam...'

> 'Robbie Schofield's mum?'
>
> 'Yes,' I reply into the mobile tucked under my chin. I am at work, tapping away on the computer, already busy with the day ahead.
>
> 'It's Cheryl from the Bulmershe School office.'
>
> I stop typing, my attention immediately focused.
>
> 'I'm calling because we were expecting Robbie at school this morning for his A level maths exam but he's not here.'
>
> 'A level maths exam?' I repeat, slow to digest. As far as I am aware, Robbie is still at home, tucked up in bed just as I left him about forty minutes ago. 'He's at home,' I tell Cheryl, adding, 'Are you sure – *sure* – he has an exam today?'
>
> 'Oh yes. Can you get him here? We tried your home number but no one picked up.'
>
> 'What time is the exam due to start?'
>
> 'About ten minutes ago.'
>
> 'Yes, I'll get him there,' I answer, flooded with panic.

I press to end the call and immediately dial home. After seven rings, I can hear the answer machine kick in.

I don't leave a message but ring Robbie's mobile. Instantly I hear, 'Robbie,' then a slight pause, 'can't come to the phone right now. Please leave a message.'

'Robbie, you need to get to school. You have an A level maths exam,' I garble down the phone. Then I try home again. No answer still.

I am stuck at work, having walked in as usual. To walk home will be a wasted half an hour and there is no one around that I can ask to drop me back.

I text Robbie, then try calling the mobile again. Such wonderful means of communication when they are switched off!

Nigey... I could try him. He might be driving, but it's worth a go.

I press 'Nigey' on my mobile and the endless unanswered ringing begins again. *What am I going to do?* I will have to try ringing the home phone incessantly until Robbie gets sick of hearing it and picks up.

I am about to punch in the number when the display starts flashing and now *my* phone is ringing. *Nigey.* 'Hello, love, did you try calling? I'm on Church Road about to drop Millie at school and had to pull over.'

I can hear the hysteria rising in my voice as I tell Nigey what's happened. Robbie hasn't had the easiest time in the sixth form and he's hardly going to help his chances by missing an entire exam.

'Stop panicking. Keep trying to ring home, and I'll turn around and head back there and get him to school.'

Quarter of an hour later, Nigey is at my office door, grinning. 'Phew, that was close,' he whistles, coming in to perch on the end of the desk. 'He doesn't do things by half, that son of yours. He was in his dressing gown watching TV, totally ignoring the phone.'

'What did he say about the exam?'

'"Oh c**p," I think were his exact words! He'd totally forgotten. Anyway, no harm done. He's the only one taking that resit so school said he will be able to have the finish time extended.'

I start to breathe again. Maybe it will be OK...

I smile at the next picture. 'This is Robs aged about three, I guess, in the garden of our old house; with all of his sit and ride vehicles – the little tractor from Argos, Noddy car, the trike, Thomas the Tank Engine. And his plastic tool kit. He loved everything about vehicles and how things worked right from the start.'

The counsellor smiles too as I pass the photo over. 'He's totally absorbed, isn't he? A little mechanic! Even got his hard hat on!'

'Yes! He couldn't wait to be able to drive the real thing! There is one particular time when I took Robbie out driving that has really stuck in my mind...'

'Please, Mum. Hopefully this is the last time.'

Taking children out whilst they are learning to drive is up there as one of the least favourite mum jobs. It is an endurance test done with gritted teeth but under the knowledge that hopefully it will be of short duration. Robbie can of course already ride his motorbike but has decided that it would be useful to be able to drive a car too. I am in complete agreement. He has had six lessons only, and his test is tomorrow.

Robbie attaches the magnetised 'L' plates and eagerly climbs in the driver's side. I, a lot less eagerly, open the passenger door. I direct him on a route round Woodley. He drives very well, very confidently. But I am still alarmed at his road positioning.

'Robbie!' I shriek, clutching my seatbelt and feeling my stomach tighten. 'We're nearly on the pavement.' The car mounts the kerb just to reiterate my point.

'Sorry.'

'Try and drive a bit further over.' I don't know whether it is because Robbie is used to different road positioning when on his bike but he will need to sort this problem out, fast.

We drive round a bit more and I start to relax a smidgen. Another half an hour and I am feeling rather good that I have done my duty as a mum; Robbie hasn't mounted the pavement again and surely that's long enough and we can head home.

'OK. Left at the roundabout and we'll head up Woodlands Avenue and back home. OK?'

'Thanks Mum.'

I watch Robbie as he glances in the rear-view mirror and indicates left. All good. He slows the car and then has to stop for traffic. The last car clears the roundabout. But as Robbie goes to pull off, I feel the car judder and stall.

'OK. Just start the engine again.' I can see a car coming up behind us.

Robbie turns the key in the ignition to restart the motor. Then I hear a brittle snapping sound and, turning, see Robbie is holding up the bunch of keys in his hand. 'The key's snapped.'

The car behind toots its horn.

'What? It can't have done!'

'Mum, the key's snapped. It's broken off in the ignition.'

I stare at my son in disbelief. I have never heard of such a thing happening. We are only about a mile from home but I resign myself to spending the next forty-five minutes sitting stuck at a roundabout waiting for the RAC to rescue us.

But next day I am delighted to get a text message from Robbie that he has passed his driving test. And my car has a new key.

There is something about Robbie and keys, I think, as we sit around the dinner table chatting and Nigey recounts his conversation with him from earlier in the day:

'What, actually down the drain? Completely down there? You can't reach to hitch them back or anything?'

'No.'

'Can you see them, even?'

'No.'

'Right. OK. Give me five mins and I'll see what I can scrabble together and come over.'

I look over at Robbie as Nigey chats away. He has finished eating, has pushed his mat forwards in the way that he does, and is sitting with his arms folded, wearing a resigned expression that says, *if you must tell everyone, let's get it over with quickly.*

'It was a good job I managed to get that mega-powerful magnet. I attached it to some wire. Pretty ingenious really.' Nigey is looking smug.

Robbie is still squirming, waiting for the teasing and laughter from the others. 'Yeah, thanks, Nige,' he says, pushing his chair back and standing up. 'Gotta go and drop the kids off at the pool.'

And he is gone. *To the loo.* I have now learnt what that particular expression of his means.

The table erupts. 'However did he manage to drop his keys down the drain? What an idiot!' Everyone is in hysterics. 'It had to be Robbie! Only Robbie could do that!'

Luckily Robbie isn't here to listen. 'Dropping the kids off at the pool' seems to have been the most sensible option, even if it has got him out of the washing up (again).

Another day I say, 'What do you mean you haven't been going in to home group? What have you been doing?'

I am sitting on the end of Robbie's bed. He is lying down, still in all his motorbike gear, minus boots and helmet. The light is off and it is getting dark outside but I can see he is pale and anxious. He has been worrying too much, overthinking, a classic family trait.

'I've just been sitting outside.'

I put my hand on his.

'But tonight, Sion came out and we chatted and I actually went in at the end.'

I tell him that I am very proud that he has managed to do this.

'I had no idea when he said he was going to Sion's home group from church, that he wasn't actually *going in.* Having outgrown the teenage group known as "Upper Room", Robbie had started attending a new church where there were a lot of young people and a much more "modern" worship style than at our old church. Now it seemed his presence outside Sion's had been noticed and he had been welcomed in. Who would have thought that from this beginning Sion would become his great friend, confidante and beer drinking buddy?'

'That's Sion there,' I say, pointing to a dark-haired chap sitting next to Robbie in the photo. 'They're in Sion's garden, sitting with Sion's son on the decking that Robbie helped to build. It's amazing to think what great friends they became.'

Robbie and I chat some more about this home group and I ask, 'I wonder how many are left in Upper Room now that you and so many have moved on?'

'Dunno. But Traidcraft is still going,' Robbie replies.

I look over at him, remembering when he was about fourteen....

'Upper Room are starting a Traidcraft stall after the service the first Sunday of every month,' Robbie informs me as he saunters into the kitchen and makes to perch himself on the edge of the kitchen side.

I am trying to cook. 'Robbie, don't sit there. I'm trying to get the tea.'

'Catherine's getting the stock.'

'That's a great thing to do. Who's doing the selling?'

'Me,' he grins. 'And the others. I guess we'll do some sort of rota. You can buy your tea and coffee and stuff from there, Mum.' And he starts reeling off figures and statistics and facts about Fairtrade as I stir the food. He has always had a great memory for facts.

'Of course I'll support you, love. Can you lay the table, please?'

He bounds up to the cutlery drawer, some song as always playing out in his head. 'Da-dee-da-da-da... Hey, it's not *meaty* pasta, is it? Again. Aww, Mum, not again, please!'

I talk to Catherine about the stall when I see her.

'You do know that it was down to Robbie that we started the Traidcraft thing, don't you?' she asks.

I *didn't* know.

'Yes, we were having a session discussing poverty and the world's resources. I told them all to get angry, *feel* angry, *be* angry about all the injustice, the inequality, the unfairness. But Robbie said he couldn't be bothered because, what difference would it make if he were angry?' She pauses and looks at me. 'I thought you knew... A couple of days later he rang me and said that he *was* angry now, *very* angry and he'd found a way to do something about it – have a Traidcraft stall. And so that's why we did. We have Robbie to thank!'

'What a great legacy to have left that church with,' the counsellor says with a smile.

'Bye, Robbie!'

The door shuts behind him. I go back into the kitchen to finish clearing up and almost immediately the doorbell rings.

Someone is charging down the stairs. 'It's only Robbie.'

'What have you forgotten?' I can hear Jack ask.

'Jus' my keys, thanks. On the stairs.'

The door shuts again and this time he is off.

SESSION 3

Rusks for Lunch

'I have so many photos of Robbie out on the water; in boats, in kayaks.' I select a picture of Robbie, proudly standing in front of his own sailing dinghy, shorts on and a loose shirt open over his T-shirt, blowing, it would seem, in the wind. Always good to have wind around when you want to sail.

> 'Hi, Robs,' I say pushing open the wooden door.
> 'Hi, Mum!'
> Robbie is sitting cross-legged on the hard floor of the Scout Hut, in shorts and a grubby T-shirt. There is a paintbrush in his hand and a pot of varnish, and before him a rather beautiful, gleaming sailing boat.
> 'Wow, love! Look at this! You've been so hard at work.'
> Robbie sets the brush down, balanced across the top of the paint pot, and stands up. 'I'll show you what I've done to it.'

'That was another restoration project performed with the utmost care and love you could lavish on a boat,' I explain to the counsellor. 'Robbie didn't just work alone; most Saturdays he had a band of Scouts to help, bribed along with the offer of free doughnuts courtesy of Robbie.'

'What a great hobby to have,' the counsellor says.

'That wasn't just an isolated project; there were many such transformations. Robbie travelled all over the country to purchase cheap sailing boats in need of TLC.'

The counsellor smiles.

'But the scouting work wasn't just restoring boats. It was a packed schedule of sailing, running camps, hiring out the teepee and fundraising.

And once a year he was down by the River Thames doing the start boat for the Regatta.'

I pass the counsellor another photo: Robbie and Jack sitting precariously balanced on what looks like a piece of fencing, out on the water of a small bay. Robbie is concentrating clearly on moving the oar. Jack looks on uncertainly.

'I often wonder where this passion for the water has come from… I had a great uncle who owned a yacht but other than that I can think of no genetic influences. Or environmental ones; after all, we hardly live near the sea.'

> I am standing on the rough tarmac outside the back of my parents' garage watching in wonder as somehow my dad and Robbie are transforming a large piece of trellis fencing into a raft – apparently. This is not at all obvious at the moment, but as I have been informed (not consulted – what would a mum know about rafts?) at every stage of the planning, design and manufacture of the craft, I know exactly what the end product will be. But I am rather anxious about several things: where will we find a suitable stretch of water to test out the raft; how will we transport the raft to the suitable stretch of water, should we find it; who will be brave enough or foolhardy enough to go with Robbie on the raft; and what if it isn't actually seaworthy, what if it sinks? My mind is racing away with itself, a long way ahead of the stage the raft is at.
>
> Robbie is standing, decked out in an old boiler suit belonging to my dad, paintbrush in hand. Grinning. It is a big operation but a realisation of one of his dreams. The rollercoaster he has drawn up plans for to go in the back garden will never progress this far (thankfully). Even Jack has been drafted in to help, and I have a deep suspicion that he is the one who will be called on to man the craft with Robbie.

'Miraculously, that raft did survive its maiden voyage in the photo,' I finish. 'But that was its one and only outing!'

I pass the counsellor another picture.

'So, where is this?' she asks.

'That's in St Ives, Cornwall. Look how long and wild Robbie's hair was then! Very hippy! And that's Jack, obviously, and they have Lottie with them, their cousin, Robbie's goddaughter. That's at her Christening. She was about two, I think.'

Robbie has two godchildren: Nate, Sion's eldest son; and Lottie, Robbie's youngest cousin. I watch as a sixteen-year-old Robbie makes his vows with the other godparents, pledging his allegiance to God and promising to help Lottie on her journey to faith. And a few years later I sit with Nigey and listen at Nate's dedication as Robbie prays over him.

Now Robbie has turned eighteen, he has been given a sizeable amount of money (which any eighteen-year-old would be delighted with) from one of his own godparents. But it comes with a challenge about using the money wisely.

Robbie opts to give all the money away to charity.

'What an amazing person he was,' the counsellor says. Then she chuckles. 'Great photo!' Robbie, arms aloft, in jeans and a black T-shirt, hair in a ponytail, is leading out the conga at his 18th. Singing.

I pass over a photo of Robbie in his motorbike gear.

'I am wondering if you find this one difficult?' the counsellor asks.

'No, not really. Riding a bike was part of who Robbie was. But it did always bring a fair amount of stress with it…'

'Hi, Robs.' It's rather late for Robbie to be ringing. He's just coming to the end of his first term at university and in a matter of days, he'll be back for the holidays.

'Hi, Mum. Promise me you won't cry.'

What kind of opening sentence is that? I am immediately gripped with panic. 'What's happened?'

'I said, promise you won't cry!'

'Yes, yes, I promise. Just tell me what's happened.'

'I've just been to hospital in an ambulance. But I'm fine.'

I sit down. 'What happened?'

It turns out that Robbie had come off his motorbike. He skidded on some wet leaves as he turned a corner. As he was going so slowly, the bike landed on top of him. Some kind person called an ambulance – but he seems OK. He has damaged his knee and scratched the bike but no other harm done.

It does no good looking back with regret. Robbie made up his mind about riding a motorbike so I made up my mind to make him as safe as possible. The hefty sum of money at Hein Gericke for all the necessary clothing, helmet and boots seems money well spent. Especially as this latest incident Robbie has just related down the phone is not the first phone call I have had along similar lines. I cast my mind back to the previous year, when he managed to slide on some oil on the road...

It is with a sense of relief that I hang up. Soon it will be the holidays and I will have Robbie back.

The counsellor smiles. 'Oh, what a brilliant picture!'

'Yes! Nigey and Robbie with the Capri. Just look at the two of them in their shades, cool as anything, leaning against the car. Like out of some '70s movie! Robbie was so happy.'

'I'm going to get a Capri.'

'What do they look like?'

Robbie finds a picture and shows me his phone.

'Are they quite old-fashioned then?'

'They're a classic car, yes, Mum.' He is used to my ignorance about most things with an engine.

Nigey understands his enthusiasm but is also concerned. 'It will eat money. We've talked about this before, Rob. Remember, I had a Capri? They're great cars but not a cheap option.'

Now Robbie has passed his test he has been borrowing my Renault Clio 1.2 when I haven't needed it. But this arrangement isn't particularly satisfactory for either of us, so he has decided to get himself a set of wheels.

There is a very narrow market for Capris in Robbie's price bracket, but he finds one for sale in Hemel Hempstead and Nigey drives him there to look it over.

'Mum, it's perfect. I've got the insurance done and I'll see you in it later!' He is on cloud nine, I can tell from his voice as he relays this information to me down the phone.

It is teeming down with rain and has been for hours. The roads must be awash and very slippery; visibility on the motorway will be poor. I am anxious, waiting at home for them both to get back, Robbie driving the newly bought Capri.

I have complete faith that Nigey wouldn't let him buy a total wreck but I am acutely aware that Robbie's budget will definitely mean a less-than-perfect car and Robbie, once his heart is set on something, can be impossible to shift.

'It feels like I'm sitting on the road!' I exclaim on my first venture in the passenger seat.

'Mum, it's meant to. It's a low-slung car!' My ignorance is exasperating Robbie.

But he soon cheers up on our return with the hardly disguised envy of the next-door neighbour as he comes out to congratulate Robbie on his new acquisition.

The Capri is the new love of Robbie's life. Like any true love, it isn't long before it is taking up a lot of Robbie's time and even more of his money. Robbie has big plans for the Capri, so big that they involve buying another cheap car so that he can transfer the drive shaft from the second car to the Capri. I am clueless about all this but it consumes a lot of Robbie's energy (and Nigey's) and means a lot of lying on his back in an old boiler suit trying to release the relevant parts.

The end result of a lot of hard graft and months of work is that the Capri doesn't have its old drive shaft but it doesn't have a new one either! It becomes a permanent fixture in the drive, a star feature on Google Earth. Robbie finds that the Ford Granada he has affectionately named 'Grandad', bought with the sole aim of using its parts, is in fact a fine old car and pretty acceptable to drive around. So, the Capri remains static in the driveway and time marches on.

'Mum can you do me a favour?'

'Hmm… depends what it is…'

'Can you be here when the guy comes to collect the Capri? I can't bear to see it go.'

It has taken a long time but Robbie has now accepted that what seems relatively straightforward in the mechanical workshop at university, with all the equipment and tools required, is rather more difficult at home. And having two cars, even if one of them doesn't function, is a luxury that as a student he can't afford. So, the Capri is being sold.

I agree to be at home. Robbie has left me with the car's official documents and strict instructions that I am to count the cash that is handed over. It is quite a big operation, as a trailer is required; after all, the car won't start.

Soon, for the first time in months, the driveway is clear right up to the garage door. I should be feeling pleased. But, surprisingly, I too am rather sad to see the Capri go.

'What I don't realise at this point is that it won't be long before the Capri is replaced by other "projects" of Robbie's that seem to fill the drive. The Capri going has simply left a void to be filled by another machine. And today, two years on from that tragic June day, we now have a Land Rover stationed there.'

'Bye, Robbie!'

The door shuts behind him. I go back into the kitchen to finish clearing up and almost immediately the doorbell rings.

Someone is charging down the stairs. 'It's only Robbie.'

'What have you forgotten?' I can hear Millie ask.

'Jus' my keys, thanks. On the stairs.'

The door shuts again and this time he is off.

Session 4

Coffee and Walnut Cake

'Hi, we're back!'

'Great timing, Mum,' Robbie calls through from the front room.

'Why?' I ask. But once in the front room I have my answer.

Robbie and his friend Groin – I never quite got to the bottom of that nickname – have been playing on the newly purchased Wii. For the moment, the controllers are abandoned on the toy box that doubles up as a coffee table amongst a lot of broken glass. Robbie has reams of blood-stained kitchen roll wound around his hand.

'I moved the controller down during the game but forgot the glass was there so I smashed it,' Robbie explains. 'Sorry, there's a lot of mess.'

On closer inspection, I realise that Robbie is quite right; it is great timing because a trip to casualty is required.

The young A & E doctor seems pathetically excited to get his 'first Wii-related injury'.

'But,' I explain to the counsellor, 'the Wii, despite that setback, is very special to us. Life had been full of the usual hassles plus the additional stress of builders at home. Robbie, back on a visit home from uni, had surprised us all. He'd handed over what was clearly a box contained in a crumpled carrier bag – he never bothered much with the pointlessness of wrapping paper!' I grin at the counsellor. 'The Wii was inside – a present for the family, generously bought with his student loan! Never mind food and books!'

I show the counsellor a photo. 'This picture just conjures up so much for me about being a family.'

The counsellor nods and smiles. 'There he is, surrounded by you all.'

'Yes,' I reply. 'I took the photo just after he had given us the Wii. Nigey, Jack, Tabby and Millie with Robbie in the middle, everyone's arms around him. And everyone looks so happy!'

Robbie is only four. The 'First Terrible Time' has started and I don't even know it yet. It is the beginning of June, a few weeks until Robbie's baby brother or sister is due. Robbie is climbing into bed next to me complaining of tummy ache.

I put my arm round him. 'You poor thing. Maybe you have a bad tummy because you're hungry...'

But he isn't hungry.

'How about doing a poo?'

But that doesn't help either.

As Robbie groans and fusses, I think how unlike him it is to whinge about anything. I don't know why, but I have a suspicion that he's got appendicitis.

The doctor we are seeing is very dismissive and even rather patronising. 'It certainly isn't appendicitis. He's got a bout of gastric flu, that's all. No need for a big drama. It will probably develop into the runs by Monday.'

It is Monday now and, strangely enough, Robbie does have the runs. But his tummy ache isn't getting any better. If anything, it seems to be hurting him more. And on Tuesday he is in so much pain that a call to the doctor is needed.

'Still bad? Right, OK, yes, I see. How old did you say? Four? Hmm... Well, he probably needs some tummy relaxant. If you can get to the Health Centre, I'll give you a prescription. It's for children over six but I think he should be fine with it.'

And now Thursday. I am sitting in the doctor's surgery. We have managed to get an emergency appointment. Thankfully, the duty doctor goes to our church and knows me well. I sit, anxiously watching, as he examines Robbie.

Then he says, 'Liz, have you got your car with you?'

I nod.

'You need to take Robbie straight to the hospital, the children's department, as I think he has a ruptured appendix. I will ring ahead and let them know you're on your way.'

The staff in the children's ward are very calming and very friendly. Within minutes they have Robbie up on the bed and are making him laugh.

The worst moment is when I have to leave him. He is with the anaesthetist and the nurse is gently easing me away and out of the room.

'Why don't you come and sit down on the ward, and I'll make you a nice cup of tea...'

But despite her kindness, I have an uncontrollable urge to get away, to leave the hospital. This is really odd because my son is here, being operated on. But I can't stay. I need to cry. I need to scream. I need to sob my heart out.

And then I am back at the hospital, back on the ward. And other children are being wheeled into the room, back after their operations; children who went to theatre after Robbie. *But Robbie isn't here.* He isn't in recovery. He is still having surgery. And I am still waiting for him, surrounded by nurses, other parents, children, visitors, but all alone...

'I remember being surprised when Robbie's nursery school teacher took this photo. I thought, "Why you would want a photo of your child in hospital?"'

I show the counsellor the picture of Robbie in the hospital bed, on a drip with a tube from his nose. He looks tiny there – lost. But he is smiling. His friend from nursery is on the bed and they are holding up toy aeroplanes.

'But we put it in a scrapbook with all the lovely cards that Robbie got then. Even his stitches are sellotaped to a page!'

'So, what was wrong?' the counsellor asks.

'Robbie didn't have a ruptured appendix (but that was removed anyway). He had a ruptured Meckel's diverticulum. A Meckel's diverticulum is something that's present in a handful of babies but mostly doesn't cause any problems. In a very small number of cases when stomach tissue is present it can secrete acid, rupture and cause ulceration. It causes severe pain and, in Robbie's case, septicaemia. I stayed eight nights with him in hospital, until he was able to eat and walk again, before he was discharged.'

I rummage through the pictures I have brought with me until I find the one of us all in Somerset for Christmas, the day after Robbie's 15th birthday. 'It wasn't a good birthday. Or Christmas,' I tell the counsellor. 'Next day, he was in hospital again.'

The 'Second Terrible Time' has started.

Strangely, the vomit looks just like red wine with no smell and definitely no diced carrots. It certainly isn't the first time Robbie has been sick like this though. As I sit with him on Christmas Day in the doctor's waiting room in Somerset where we are staying, I think back over several other such occasions.

The surgery door opens and the doctor comes out. 'Come in now, please.' Then, inside, he begins rather patronisingly, 'So, young man, what's the problem?'

I listen as Robbie tells the doctor that he awoke yesterday (his birthday) to bad stomach pains and then he started being sick; and that it's still just the same today so we called the out-of-hours medical service and they booked us into this surgery.

The doctor examines Robbie and I add, 'He had a ruptured Meckel's diverticulum when he was four and also had his appendix out at the same time.'

The doctor is nodding and listening to Robbie's stomach with his stethoscope; then, the next minute, he is dismissing us out of the door with the words 'tummy upset' and 'plenty of fluids'.

It is clear to me that it is not just a 'tummy upset'. Robbie hasn't been interested in any of the Christmas fuss and is still in pain. So, by Christmas evening, we are at Yeovil A & E Department.

'No bowel sounds,' the young registrar announces. 'That's not good. It means that nothing is getting through to your bowel so there must be a blockage somewhere. You're going to need to go up to the ward and we'll put you on a drip.'

The porter has, he tells us, been on duty since 7am that morning and now it is almost midnight. The nurse also chats to me about her day as I perch on the edge of Robbie's bed, holding his hand and trying with all my power not to faint as a tube is passed down his nose and into his stomach.

The idea, we are told, is to drain Robbie's tummy in the hope that when it is empty, it will be able to free itself from the scar tissue it has become 'hooked on' from the operation when he was four. This process, the registrar adds, could take several days, but he hopes to be able to avoid another operation which will only make more scar tissue.

'I stayed in hospital with Robbie again. Three nights. Luckily the scar tissue did unhook itself and he was discharged.'

'What difficult times...' the counsellor says.

'Ah, this is nice,' Nigey says stretching his arm out and around my shoulders, both of us totally oblivious that this is the start of the 'Third Terrible Time'.

We are sitting in bed having a cup of tea before getting up for church when the phone rings. I reach out quickly to answer it; the phone doesn't usually ring at this time on a Sunday morning.

'Hello? Is that Rob Schofield's mother?'

'Yes,' I say, not recognising the man's voice.

Beside me, Nigey sits up and swings his legs off the bed.

'I'm Scott. I'm one of the leaders at the Outdoor Education Centre where your son Rob is staying.'

I clutch the phone. Robbie is away on an outwards-bound weekend with his course at university.

'I'm ringing because Rob was admitted to Barrow-in-Furness Hospital last night with stomach pains and vomiting.'

I hear a small gasp escape. Nigey leans in to try and hear what the man is saying.

'I haven't spoken to the hospital yet this morning but of course I will do later. I wanted to let you know so that you can call them if you like and talk to Rob. I still have his mobile and all his things here.'

'Yes, of course. Thank you.' My voice is small and shaky.

When I make the call, the nurse isn't very friendly and tells me that Robbie was admitted through A & E, that he was in some pain but is reasonably comfortable now and has stopped being sick. She begrudging-ly lets me have a quick chat with him.

'I knew straight away what was wrong, Mum. Scott thought it was too much alcohol but I didn't have anything to drink. I basically said he had to take me to hospital.'

'I'll come up straight away, love.'

'Don't rush. I feel a lot better than last night and it's a long drive.'

Soon I have driven the 286 miles to Barrow-in-Furness General Hospital.

'It's not visiting time,' the nurse informs me very bluntly.

'Yes, I know. I'm sorry, but I have just driven up from Reading and would like to see my son – and like someone to tell me what's wrong.'

'Constipation. He'll be right as rain soon.'

'Constipation?' I am dumbfounded. Robbie has never suffered with this. 'But that wouldn't have made him sick...'

The nurse is giving me a disdainful look. 'I'm sure you understand that everything needs to be taken into consideration and examined. The consultant will be round again tomorrow but for the moment we are treating him for constipation.'

A few days later they have decided that it isn't constipation. It's another bowel blockage. Eight hours after his barium meal, it still hasn't passed through Robbie's system and he vomits it back up again. There is going to have to be another operation. I send up lots of prayers.

'Robbie was nineteen and deemed an adult, so I wasn't allowed to see him before the operation as it wasn't visiting time. And Robbie wasn't meant to use his mobile phone. The nurse told me what time Robbie would be going to theatre so that I could ring and talk to him before then. But when I called, I was told that I'd missed him and he'd already gone down. I was so upset that I was too late. Of course, I had no awareness of the future then, how in only seven years' time I would be too late again. And never have another chance.' I blow my nose. 'The consultant, though, was as good as his word and called me as soon as the operation was done. Robbie's bowel had been strangled by scar tissue and reduced to a third of its size. He had to cut into the bowel itself, so Robbie also had internal stitches. Apparently, bowel obstructions and strangulations are very serious. Once the blood supply to the bowel is cut off, sections start to die. In some cases, without emergency treatment it can lead to death. Thankfully, God pulled Robbie through. Then.'

After listening to the story, the counsellor continues to look through the photographs and then comments on one. 'This is a happy photo. So many of you! Looks like someone's birthday...'

'Yes. It's Jack's 18th – all of the family out in the pub. Robbie had been away and travelled back to join us for lunch.'

We are already at the pub when Robbie swings in, smiling and relaxed.

'Happy birthday, Stick,' he calls to Jack, taking the empty seat at the crowded table.

'Got you a beer, Rob,' Nigey says pushing the glass down to Robbie's place. 'How'd you get on?'

'Yeah, awesome thanks! We actually didn't do too badly!'

Robbie has been at Silverstone in my little red Clio. He tells me with great pride how my little car has been on the starting grid there and done a whole lap. (Yes, it actually made it all the way around! What he fails to mention are all the handbrake turns that he has been doing in it too...) He has been taking part in a Formula Student event. Formula Student, run by the Institution of Mechanical Engineers, is an annual competition for universities around the world to design, build and test a racing car. Helping to build the car has mostly been a pleasurable experience and Robbie has devoted a substantial amount of his limited free time to the construction of it.

From a little boy, Robbie has always loved designing and building. For a long time, he has wanted to become a mechanical and automotive engineer. He is in the last year at Birmingham, just finishing his Master's degree with a job offer at McLaren under his belt. It is his dream job.

Or it *was* his dream job. It seems only a short time later that Robbie is telling us he has changed his mind. He feels called to become a teacher rather than pursuing a career on the track side. He will finish his masters and do a PGCE, trusting in what he believes God is calling him to do.

'Bye, Robbie!'

The door shuts behind him. I go back into the kitchen to finish clearing up and almost immediately the doorbell rings.

Nigey's voice calls, 'It's only Robbie.'

'What have you forgotten, Robs?'

'Jus' my keys, thanks. On the stairs. Oh, and my wallet.'

The door shuts again and this time he is off.

Session 5

Steak and Ale Pie

Today, I watch as Robbie is playing air drums walking up the drive on his way back from putting out the rubbish. One of the others at an upstairs window bangs on the glass at him. They switch between teasing him as any sibling would and getting exasperated at the constant drumming on the table at meals or at the *tum-tum-tum* noise that is just audible under his breath.

'Having fun?' I laugh as he comes into the front room, not able to help myself and being no better than the others.

'Ha, ha!' He sits down, playing on his phone, and I think he must be totally absorbed when he comes out with, 'Anyway, it's all your fault.'

As a mother, I am quite used to hearing that everything that has gone wrong in the entire world somehow or other comes down to being my fault. 'What is?'

'The drums. You started it when I was little with the saucepan lids.'

The saucepan lids... Ah, yes! He is right after all. The saucepan lids were definitely my fault. I was a young mum, only twenty when Robbie was born and full of childishness myself. Money was tight, but I was resourceful. The 'drum kit' recipe involved a lot of string, a clothes airer, two wooden spoons and the saucepan lids. It was heaven for Robbie but hell, no doubt, for the neighbours.

'He looks so cool!' the counsellor laughs, holding up another picture.

'Yes. He was about nine or ten then, I suppose. Been learning the clarinet. He was part of a jazz band they had at school for a while. He's wet his hair and slicked it back and got his sunglasses on!' I smile as happy memories come flooding back.

'So, can I learn, Mum?' Robbie's enthusiasm is infectious.

'OK then,' I laugh, 'why not? But you will have to practise every day and that means even when you don't feel like it.'

'Yeah, I will. Course I will.'

And that's what's brought us to the music shop in Taplow to purchase a clarinet. It's not my area of expertise; I'm a strings person, a violinist. But someone has been to school and played the clarinet and encouraged the pupils to have lessons; and this promotion has clearly had an effect on my son and a couple of his friends.

The clarinet is purchased and the lessons begin. Robbie is diligent at first and I try to block out the squawks and squeaks that seem to fill every room of the house at practice time, in the relief that he actually is practising and, so far, the expensive purchase hasn't been a waste of money.

'The cloth's stuck. I can't pull it either way,' Robbie is calling through the open kitchen doorway to me, clarinet in hand.

'Robbie, it can't be stuck.' I put down the dishcloth and take the instrument from him. There are the rather frayed ends of a cleaning cloth protruding from the bottom end of the clarinet. Robbie has always been very zealous in cleaning out the spit after each practice, but now, unbelievably, the cloth has actually got wedged in the main section of the clarinet and won't budge. I give another exasperated tug and a few stray strands of thread come off in my hand, but nothing more. 'You'll have to take it to show your teacher. Your lesson's tomorrow anyway.' I hand the instrument back and it gets packed away again in the case.

But after school next day, Robbie announces, 'Mr Edwards couldn't get the cloth out either, Mum. He said it's caught on the other side of one of the keys. He thinks we'll have to take it back to the shop.'

I sigh. Another trip out to Taplow then.

'I've never seen a problem like this before.' The young man in the music shop in Taplow is stroking his chin and looking thoughtful.

Please, please don't say we have to buy another clarinet. I send my prayer up and try to look hopeful.

Robbie is having a good look round. He seems to have his eye on a lot of other instruments too. We need to leave this shop promptly before I end up re-mortgaging the house...

'The only thing I can think of trying is to burn the cloth out.'

'Oh, my goodness! But won't that damage the instrument?' I am horrified.

Robbie is back at my side in a flash. He clearly likes the sound of the fire a lot more than I do. But we are not going to be allowed to see this procedure. Robbie is disappointed; I am still praying.

'There you go.' The young man is smiling now and handing the clarinet back. 'All done. Good as new. Should be fine. You'll have to buy another cleaning cloth, though.'

Luckily this just means I stump up a bit of cash rather than write a cheque and we are soon back in the car on the way home.

'Mum, if it happens again, can I burn the cloth out myself?'

'No, no and no! Just try not to make so much spit when you play so you don't have to clean it so often.'

We grin at each other.

'The clarinet was joined by a tenor sax and countless guitars. Robbie was part of "The Retweets" band with some of his close friends. They played in the local pub, at various weddings and charity events, and despite hectic lives, still fitted in time to practise and play in the church worship band. Robbie loved his music – could turn his hand to pretty much anything. And he loved composing too.

'But there was something about his twelve-string guitar. It was a "gift" from one of Robbie's uncles, an unwanted guitar with a broken neck – but Nigey mended it, Robbie mastered it and it became my favourite thing to hear him playing. Metallica's "Nothing Else Matters" and Led Zeppelin's "Stairway to Heaven". The music, played across all the strings, was a wonder to watch, a joy to hear. There was something about it that moved me, that captured me, that spoke to my heart.'

Finally, the kitchen is looking beautiful. The extension has at last been completed, the flooring is down and the walls are a very pale light-reflecting blue. In the soft glow of the candles in the Advent crown, it does indeed look perfect.

'Robs, d'you want a glass of mulled wine?' I ask as he sits in the dining room part, at the piano.

'Yeah, go on then. Thanks.'

I carry the warm glass through. 'I'll put it here for you on top of the piano.'

'Awesome! Thanks.' Robbie has the ancient carol book open that belonged to my sister years ago. But he has never had lessons and has just worked out himself what the notes are and how to play.

I am just leaving the kitchen when the strains of 'Good King Wenceslas' are interrupted with a screech of chair legs on the wooden floor, the unmistakable sound of breaking glass and an 'Oh, c**p' from Robbie.

I turn back. There, across the whole expanse of the newly painted wall to the right of the piano, is a splattering of red wine, like huge ink blots and running streams.

'It just slipped. Sorry, Mum.'

There is nothing to be done that will shift the stain except to completely repaint the wall...

A little while later he tells me, 'Adam's asked me and Ryan to be joint best man.'

'Oh, that's lovely, Robbie. And that's two of you to share the responsibility of the stag do!'

Ryan comes around to plan the stag party with Robbie. They are dividing the jobs up and it falls on Robbie to book the accommodation.

Several weeks on, the day in question arrives. Some of the men are arriving at our house to meet before heading off to the south coast to put Adam through his paces. I am standing chatting in the back room to Adam's dad when Adam comes in.

'Just a pre-warning,' he announces to the room, grinning widely, 'but for this all-male stag do, it looks like Robbie has booked all double rooms. To share. Cosy!'

There is a general burst of laughter and Robbie enters sheepishly. 'I expect no one will care after the evening we've got planned.'

I smile to myself as I wave them off. Only Robbie could manage to book double beds for an all-male party.

'But of course, it was all fine and it ended up being another good story to tell. A bit like the eve of the wedding itself.'

The counsellor nods and smiles as she holds the photo in her hand: Robbie at Adam's wedding.

Robbie has been out the night before with Adam and has come back entrusted with his suit and shoes. But as I pull back the curtains on the morning of the wedding, I am struck by something hanging down from the roof of Robbie's Land Rover parked out in the cul-de-sac. No, surely it can't be... It can't be *Adam's suit?* But as I lean forwards to get a better look, I realise that not only is Adam's wedding suit hanging from the outside of the Land Rover, but his shoes are perched on top of it too.

'Robbie, Robbie! You are *so* lucky it didn't rain last night.'

'What? Why?'

He is in his fleecy blue dressing gown, wearily rubbing the sleep from his eyes.

'Look outside!'

'Oh, c**p!' And he is off tearing down the drive into the cul-de-sac, the laces of his trainers flying, to retrieve the precious items. 'I remember taking the suit and shoes out of the Land Rover, then I must have put them down to lock the door and totally forgotten to pick them up again.'

'Anyway,' I say to reassure him, 'Adam will never know. And thankfully it didn't rain and they weren't nicked.' I give him a big smile. 'Just the speech to worry about and it'll all be over.'

'Frankie and Benny's. Robbie's 23rd birthday. There was a water leak at TGI's so we went there instead.'

There are balloons in the photo – a group shot of all of us and Robbie's girlfriend. It was the first time I was aware that he had a problem eating.

'Sorry, I just can't eat this. My back's really bad.'

Robbie can't eat his steak but I am not unduly worried. Robbie doesn't live with us, I don't see him eat every day; I am sure it is just a one-off.

But over the next couple of months, Robbie mentions a few times about his back pain and decides to see the doctor. The text that I get afterwards from my son isn't exactly complementary about the doctor. Contrary to what Robbie thinks should happen, he is referred to a gastro specialist.

Soon, on the advice of the consultant, we are at the hospital waiting for Robbie to have a gastroscopy. Robbie has opted to be partly sedated for this, so I have come along too to drive him home.

'OK, young man, time to come through.'

I settle back with my book and hope that Robbie is faring alright. I have managed to read quite a few chapters before he emerges, looking slightly giddy, and sits on the chair next to me.

'How did it go, love?'

'Well, it's not fun.'

'Are you OK to go now?'

'No, they want to talk to us. I think they said something about an ulcer.'

'An *ulcer?* Are you sure?'

'Think so.'

We wait companionably for a while. Robbie has his 'Total Guitar' to read and I continue with my book.

'Robbie, Robbie's Mum. Could you come through so that the consultant can have a word please?'

What follows puts me into total shock. Robbie is still very woozy and not really taking everything in, but it transpires that Robbie has a condition known as Barrett's oesophagus. I have never heard of it before.[3] He has a 10cm length area of damaged cells, which is nearly half his oesophagus affected, and he also has two ulcers.

The consultant has taken thirteen biopsies and we need to make another appointment for two weeks' time when he will take more. 'Just to be on the safe side.' He is amazed that Robbie hasn't had more trouble eating.

A few weeks later, Robbie, Nigey and I are back at the hospital. The consultant has taken a total of eighteen biopsies and, staggeringly, as an answer to prayer, they are all benign. Robbie will be on medication for life and need regular gastroscopies to monitor his condition.

As I learn more about Barrett's oesophagus and gastro reflux disease, I start to question why this wasn't picked up earlier. The consultant tells me that he thinks Robbie probably started with this problem when he was about ten. I think of all the trouble he has had, frequently being sick and the bowel blockages meaning stuff can only go back up instead of down. And I think of all the occasions I took him to the doctors with unexplained sore throats and, at one point, a problem with excess burping. But these latter things were dismissed and I rather suspect 'paranoid mother' was written on Robbie's medical notes.

It is as I'm glancing, rather absentmindedly, through a round robin leaflet from Cancer Research that the words 'Barrett's' and 'oesophageal cancer' and 'new treatment' jump out at me. I google the man whom the article refers to and find an email address.

I want to get Robbie on the bandwagon for this treatment if I possibly can. So, the email is sent and before long I have a reply that the man would like my phone number and to chat to me. I am slightly thrown that the thick Scottish accent doesn't match the Polish name, but the man is very interested in Robbie's case and clearly wants to help. He tells me that as a male, over twenty-

[3] I read afterwards that reflux from stomach acid can cause cells in the oesophagus to become abnormal, carrying a risk of turning cancerous.

five, white and with 10cm of affected oesophagus, Robbie is high risk. He also tells me that whilst he isn't a medical doctor, he will put me in touch with someone in Portsmouth who is an expert in this field. He duly does this and the Portsmouth doctor emails to say he would like to treat Robbie. All Robbie has to do is to get a referral from the GP.

'This was the process that Robbie was going through when he was called to his eternal dwelling. Circumstances have intervened. Robbie will now definitely not get oesophageal cancer.'

'Bye, Robbie!'

The door shuts behind him. I go back into the kitchen to finish clearing up and almost immediately the doorbell rings.

Someone is charging down the stairs. 'It's only Robbie.'

'What have you forgotten?' I can hear Tabby ask.

'Jus' my keys, thanks. On the stairs.'

The door shuts again and this time he is off.

Session 6

Dime Bars and Freddos

It is really very useful, I think to myself, to have a son who is confident and happy to drive me to the supermarket in this deep snow. Otherwise, if I had walked, I wouldn't have been able to buy nearly as much.

Robbie is excited about the snow. He keeps chains and a spade in the back of his Land Rover, and as we drive home, he is busy recounting to me all the stories of people he has helped this week, digging their cars out of the snow, or giving them a tow. He doesn't see it as an imposition but is pleased that he has the kind of vehicle that he can utilise to help people out.

We pull into our long drive. Nigey has put salt down so the snow isn't too bad here. But our elderly neighbours, whose drive is equally as long as ours, and wider, haven't been able to clear their snow. So, armed with spades and shovels, we head round and set to, clearing away the snow from their drive and piling it into the wheelbarrow to deposit in the centre of the cul-de-sac on the grass 'roundabout'. Before long, others in the road are out too, and soon, as a joint venture, we manage to shift the snow from the cul-de-sac too, so the road is clear up to the main section of the street.

'Right,' Robbie announces when it's all done. 'I'm off round to Sion's to help board his attic. See you later.'

'He was so generous with his time and so happy to help others.'

The counsellor leans over and takes the photo from my hand of a four-year-old Robbie, big cheeky smile, crouching down in front of a stunning display of tulips.

'That time in Holland always brings back this memory...'

'Robbie, whatever are you doing?'

We are in Holland, in Rockanje to be exact, as a family for a four-month secondment.

'Sending my Lego to the children,' Robbie answers, absorbed in his task, wrapping individual pieces of Lego in little pieces of paper and Sellotape.

We haven't taken much with us to Holland – well, a carload but that doesn't mean many toys. And Lego is Robbie's all-time tip-top favourite. The TV, showing us BBC1 and BBC2, is in our only liveable room so that means Robbie has often been around when the news has been on. I haven't realised it has had an impact on him; he is only just four.

'Which children?' I ask him. But I already know the answer.

'Those ones on telly. The poor children. The sad ones. This'll make them happy again.'

I picture the Kosovan children fleeing their homes with their families, heading out into the unknown in a desperate attempt to escape. How wonderful if they could be made happy by receiving one piece of Lego each, inexpertly wrapped and sent via magic to the middle of nowhere. How lovely to have that child's sense of innocence. But also, how remarkable that my own child has such a conscience at this tender age and a need to do something to alleviate their pain.

'Oh, sweetheart, that's a really kind thing to do,' I smile.

Afterwards, when he has gone to bed, I will unwrap the pieces and put them back with the rest of his Lego and pretend they have been sent.

'What fun!' the counsellor exclaims looking at the photo of Robbie on a summer holiday in Belgium. He is in his mid-teens and sitting on the beach, T-shirt pulled up over his face, sunglasses on over his T-shirt. It's the sunglasses that make the picture.

Robbie has started wearing glasses – not the usual prescription lens sort but glasses with clear lenses. They are part of his teaching 'uniform'. I don't know how this has happened or who has given him the idea, but he is at UEA doing his PGCE wearing costume glasses.

'I've started to share lifts to school and back with Emma as she's got her teaching practice in the same place,' he tells me down the phone.

'That's good. What does she teach?'

'Geography – so basically colouring in. It was so funny the other day. I'd gone in the Land Rover and I was giving Emma a lift. At the end of the day she got in and I started the engine. Then, before I drove away, I took my glasses off and put them in my top pocket. Emma looked at me and then she says, "Err, don't you need those for driving? Most people put their glasses on when they get behind a wheel. You've just taken yours off!"'

'Robbie! I hope you told her. I hope you said that they were just for show. Poor girl!'

'Nah, I just said I was OK driving without them!'

'Robbie!'

'But I'm gonna have to get a new pair now. I was walking through the playground with Steve, and the kids were out playing football, and the ball comes flying through the air towards us, hits me, knocks my glasses off and breaks them. Steve went ballistic at the kids, said that Mr Schofield won't be able to function without those, etcetera. It was really funny.'

'I hope you told him not to worry – that they aren't real...'

'Nah! I couldn't do that cos he'd wonder why I was wearing them. He was so worried how I would be able to see without them. Classic!'

The glasses do get replaced but when Robbie comes to Reading for the interview for his first teaching job, the glasses get forgotten. And after that, he finds that he doesn't need to wear them to teach after all. He can do a perfectly good job without them.

'This is hilarious! Look,' I say, showing the counsellor a photo of the six of us under a leaden grey sky, coats on. Tabby is even wearing her woolly hat. 'We are on our summer holiday, though from the weather, you would never believe that it's August!'

Today the rain is so torrential that even the short walk into the centre of Swanage is likely to get us drenched through. So, instead, we take two cars and park in the town. Nigey and I are planning to mooch around the shops but the others decide to head to the arcade and whittle away the morning and a lot of loose change. Robbie is heading straight for the 2p coin pusher machines.

'There's a lot of attractive prizes,' I joke to him glancing over the array of plastic novelties laid out to tempt people to part with their cash. 'Although, having said that, the billiard ball keyring actually *is* nice.'

Nigey and I head off and leave the others to it. The rain isn't easing. It's lashing against the buildings and making even mooching in the shops a miserable affair.

Soon it's lunchtime and we have all met up again in one of the town centre pubs, along with a lot of other damp holidaymakers.

'Oh, Mum, before I forget, I got this for you,' Robbie says, and he lays down on the table in front of me an olive green billiard ball keyring – from the arcade.

I am speechless. I thought Robbie had realised I was being sarcastic. But evidently not. 'Oh, sweetheart, you didn't have to do that! How many 2p coins did you have to feed into the machine to win it?'

'Argh, not much. 'bout three pounds. But it was worth it – you said you liked it.' He shrugs his shoulders.

And I am still speechless. Three pounds for that worthless bit of plastic! Yet I am incredibly touched that Robbie has spent his morning and three pounds all for me.

The next day reveals a weak sun struggling against the racing clouds.

'We should get out on the bikes, as we made the effort to bring them,' Nigey announces at breakfast.

It always takes a lot longer than we plan for, getting six bikes out and ready for the off. There always seems to be at least one flat tyre. Eventually we are away, though, cycling up the hill in the direction of the country park. It's tough-going and the clouds seem to be winning as a slow steady drizzle sets in.

Jack is first to the park gates. 'It says no cycling,' he informs us.

It is going to be one of those days...

With the weather miserable and the park a no-go, we decide to head back down the hill into Swanage for some lunch. Progress is much faster going down. I struggle to keep up with the others racing ahead, so I'm not with Nigey when he comes spectacularly off his bike on the steep road, but I see it happening.

It is Robbie who is first there, Robbie who follows Nigey as he slowly gets back up and starts for home, Robbie who goes after him, Robbie who makes sure he is alright.

Robbie and two of his friends are standing decked out in oversized navy-blue uniforms in Sol Joel car park by the school. 'His first day at school,' I explain to the counsellor. They are grinning, squirming a bit from the bright sun. 'He was so cute!'

It seems incredible that Robbie is now teaching. Surely, it can't be all those years since he started school himself?

There is stuff everywhere. *At one point,* I think to myself, *you used to be able to see the carpet in here.* Now the flooring consists of books, paper, homework, clothes, pens, Freddo wrappers, a battery and much more. This is the mark of a genius at work: Mr Schofield, science teacher extraordinaire.

'What's this about?' I bend down and pick up a piece of paper, clearly a pupil's work with drawings of what seem to be Mr Men all over.

'Oh, that's for genetics,' Robbie says, glancing over. 'It's easier to explain like that: looking at the Mr Men's characteristics and then seeing what you get if you, say, cross Mr Greedy with Mr Happy – a yellow Mr Man with a big belly!'

'Sounds like fun. Great idea.'

'Look.' He turns around on his drum stool that doubles as a desk chair and looks at his Mac. 'This is what I was doing yesterday with Year 10. It's about sound waves.'

I wait while he opens up the right window. Suddenly there is music, something rocky, and I can see a line across the screen, fire and, as the music begins to notch up a gear, the fire dances up and down, increasing as the music gets louder.

'It's a Ruben's Tube,' he explains. 'It helps them to understand the acoustic waves. Cos of the music and fire and stuff, it sticks in their mind and helps them remember.'

He is a hands-on teacher, believing that you learn through doing. And although I am biased, I can see that his lessons are great fun. I think back to the little experiments that I used to do with Robbie before he started school, mainly involving water and a lot of mess; it's much more fun to mix two things together yourself and see the result than read about it in a book.

'Bye, Robbie!'

The door shuts behind him. I go back into the kitchen to finish clearing up.

'Count to ten,' Jack says – and on cue the doorbell rings. 'What have you forgotten?' he asks opening the door.

'Jus' my keys, thanks. On the stairs.'

The door shuts again and this time he is off.

SESSION 7

Christmas Pud

'There are some lovely photos here.'

'Yes. Important reminders of how there can be happy times in the midst of difficulties. That holiday was just after Nigey's dad had died. We came back to his funeral. But despite that, and despite Millie ending up in hospital on holiday with food poisoning, we did have a lot of fun.'

> It is 'corking hot'. I guess that's Cyprus in late July. We are all here on holiday, even Robbie who is now in his twenties. Just for a week. The journey here has been uneventful, except for a sense of déjà vu at the airport…
>
> 'Is this your bag, young man?' the guy scanning the hand luggage in the security hall asks Robbie.
>
> 'Yeah. That's mine.'
>
> The guy opens up the bag. It's Robbie's 'school bag', the one he stores all his things in for teaching.
>
> 'You can't take these on board.' A pair of scissors are retrieved from within and held up.
>
> 'Robbie! Whatever are you doing with those?'
>
> Robbie shrugs. 'Guess they were just in my bag for school. I didn't think to check it first; just shoved a few extra things in for the holiday.'
>
> The scissors are placed in the bin behind the security man and we are allowed to proceed. But it brings back memories of the penknife incident a few years before and Nigey saying, 'Right, ready folks?' ushering us forwards. 'Final check, no one has anything they shouldn't have?' We had all shaken our heads then, even Robbie, until he had put his hands in his shorts pocket to

check. 'Oh, c**p. I've got my penknife.' 'Robbie!' 'I last wore these shorts to Scouts.' He shrugged. 'Guess I must've left it in there.'

Now I say, 'That's twice. *Twice,* Robbie! No blades on the plane!'

He isn't rattled, simply shrugs again and we move on.

All is forgotten now we have arrived. The villa is perfect: lovely pool, air conditioning, near restaurants and the beach.

'Right, I'm going to go in and get a shower,' I announce to a pool full of husband and kids, in an effort to channel them all into getting a shower too so that we can head out for something to eat.

As I finish drying myself and chuck the towel in the *en suite,* Robbie saunters in to the cool of my bedroom.

'Shall we check out that Japanese restaurant tonight?' he asks, leaning back against the wall under the air conditioning. 'It's one of those places where they have a hot plate and cook at your table and do tricks and things. Looked good when we went past the other day, and it does teriyaki chicken and stuff so there'll be something that everyone likes. Look.' He holds out his phone so I can see the screen. 'This is the menu.'

I can't believe he hasn't noticed: I am standing fresh from my shower, completed naked, and Robbie hasn't even batted an eyelid. 'Well love, I could look now when I am completely starkers, or we could carry this conversation on when I've got dressed.'

'Oh, c**p.' In a split second, he has screwed up his face, shut his eyes and, just for good measure, thrown his hand across. Then he walks out through the door. 'Later. Or I'll be psychologically scarred for life. Thanks, Mum.'

We are back home.

'Robbie's here!' Millie is shouting down from her bedroom at the front.

Next minute, I can hear keys in the door, a thud, footsteps and my son appears in the kitchen doorway. I'm busy with the Friday night tea and, as he often does, Robbie has called by on his way to Scouts. I go over and fill up the kettle.

'Hi, love. How are you?'

'Good,' he grins. 'How are you?'

'Yeah, OK. What's new?'

'Bit of drama this morning when the ceiling fell in.' He is smiling at me, waiting for my reaction.

'The ceiling fell in! What d'you mean? At school?'

'Yeah. I was, like, teaching the window lickers, second period, that's always mega on a Friday as they're already in weekend mode; and Scot starts on about some crack on the ceiling, but we carry on; and then there's this massive crash from upstairs and suddenly the ceiling smashes in and water comes pouring down.'

'Oh, my days, Robbie! Was anyone hurt?'

'Nah! It was awesome. We had to move into another lab. Glad I don't have to sort the mess. Thanks, Mum.'

I hand him a mug of tea. I love hearing about his teaching stories. And the poor 'window lickers', that I know he has a soft spot for; it's for them that he has gone into teaching, after all.

'How's that boy who got stabbed in the hand?'

'What, that one during the heart dissection, d'you mean? The one that got a scalpel through his hand?'

'Yes,' I laugh, although it's not really a funny subject. 'Yes, I do mean that one. How many stabbings do you have?'

'Ha, ha. Yeah, he's OK, but he's not with me now – moved to the other Rob's class to keep him and Jason apart.' He sets down his mug. 'Better go. Won't see you next Friday, Mum. Away all weekend with Duke of Edinburgh. Straight after school Friday to Sunday evening.'

'That's tough, love. That's like two full weeks of work with no break. Will text you.'

'Robbie was able to relate so well to his teenaged pupils. He'd been through difficult times himself in his teens,' I explain to the counsellor.

Being a teenager isn't easy. There are things that Robbie is struggling with. It is a difficult day for everyone when he confides in us about exactly how bad he is feeling and that he can't manage these feelings any more. But I am so thankful that he has been brave enough to share some things with us and ask for help. And I am also thankful that I am able to find him some help.

One of the people who is part of the Christian Meditation group I attend is a counsellor and I call her up, trusting that she will be able to advise me and point me to the best source of help. Within a couple of weeks Robbie is having one-to-one counselling sessions.

I start the process of finding Robbie a place at a different school for the sixth form. This happens very swiftly and in a couple of days Robbie has moved to the same school that the others attend. The counselling doesn't produce such quick results and Robbie only has a few sessions. But he has his trusty blue NIV hardback Bible. It is covered in his writing and sticky notes; it pulls him through.

I hand the counsellor a picture of Robbie's beloved Land Rover and recall another cherished memory.

It has been utterly transformed, this 'new' Land Rover Defender, a slightly more up-to-date model bought to replace the old one. Who would have thought that this trusty (well, mostly) old vehicle so beloved by my son could have metamorphosed into a glamorous golden carriage? There are gold ribbons wound round the door handles, across the bonnet and over the boot. No other vehicle could have been more apt or more wonderfully loved to transport Robbie's grandparents from home to church for the blessing to celebrate their 50th wedding anniversary. But Robbie has only just arrived in time. It has been the usual last minute of panic and stress and hurried preparations – the signs of a life lived to its fullest in which every minute can be accounted for and each is precious.

The counsellor smiles at the photo of the Land Rover in its glorious golden state. Robbie has his back to the camera, helping my mum down from the vehicle. But it is a clever picture, taken by Jack. You can see Robbie's broad smile reflected in the Land Rover's window.

'What a special picture.'

'This is the day which the Lord has made; let us rejoice and be glad in it.'

We are in church now. The pews are full; family from all corners of the country, friends from just as afar and even one of my parents' bridesmaids from Germany. Robbie is at the lectern reading words that my parents have chosen and asked him, as eldest grandchild, to read.

'We say, "When I get married..." "When we move into a new house..." "When the children start school..." "When I haven't the old folks to look after..." Have you ever thought how much time and energy we spend longing for some time in the near or distant future when we think that life will really begin or that circumstances will be more congenial?'

He has a clear, strong voice – a teacher's confidence, after all; beautiful diction. His hair has been newly cut and he is sporting his usual stubble on a face fresh with a healthy summer glow. And a shirt with his jeans! I am pleased; he looks so lovely in a shirt.

My eyes drift from Robbie and across to the stained-glass window at the side. This elegant and wonderfully crafted church is so familiar to me from my teens, with its simple stonework and striking paintings of St Peter. There is a stained-glass window behind the altar and only one other, this one to the side. Crouching down with the shepherds at the front is Simon, the son of a previous vicar, killed in a hit-and-run accident aged only five. I remember when it happened, and when the window was installed.

'Back then,' I tell the counsellor, 'I had no awareness of the devastation, the heart-ripping grief, the sorrow, the struggle to carry on that they must all have faced. Thinking of Robbie and what we've been through, I wish with the most intense passion that I could've been spared having that sense of shared understanding now. But on that day, my parents' wedding anniversary, I had no idea of what the future had in store, what few years Robbie would have to fill.'

'Sometimes, we are planning to enjoy ourselves without some of the ties and difficulties that make present life a burden. Sometimes we may genuinely be looking forward to a time when we think we shall be able to serve God more actively. Whatever our motive, we're waiting for the future in order to live,' Robbie is saying, looking around at his audience, at his grandparents in the front row and all the rest of us behind them.

This has never been Robbie's problem, I think. He is one of life's doers; he has already packed his life full.

'But... every new day, with its potential for happiness and sadness, high drama or dull routine, is a gift from God. Knowing that whatever comes is known to him, we can receive and use it with thankful hearts. This is the day which the Lord has made; let us rejoice and be glad in it.'

What poignant words.

'Bye, Robbie!'

The door shuts behind him. I go back into the kitchen to finish clearing up and almost immediately the doorbell rings.

I go through the hall to answer it. 'Hi, Robbie. What have you forgotten, love?'

'Jus' my keys, thanks, and my jacket. On the stairs.'

The door shuts again and this time he is off.

SESSION 8

Banana Bread and Pineapple

I am sitting at home, in the back room to be precise, relaxing with Nigey, when the text comes through; I have been expecting it all afternoon. It simply reads, 'She said yes!'

I text Robbie back, congratulating him and welcoming his fiancée to the family. The ring was bought some time ago and has been sitting, until a few days ago, in our safe. Robbie has shared his plans with us, told us about the trip to the seaside, and has now popped the question.

The counsellor looks at the photo of us all out together with them both in a restaurant, celebrating their engagement.

A while after this, we are all out in the countryside – Robbie and his fiancée and both sets of parents – to view the proposed reception venue. It is a very beautiful old barn and Robbie has plans of a bouncy castle and a pick and mix out on the lawn. I think back to all those parties, every year for about fourteen years, with a bouncy castle in the back garden at home. All those happy memories. And although he does later change his mind, I feel glad that Robbie must share those memories too.

'A line of boys!' I exclaim looking at the picture. 'Robbie must be about ten. Probably his last Cub camp. He was always so filthy when he got home. He so loved camping; went on so many Cub and Scout camps. But his life was moving on…'

Weekends taken up with Duke of Edinburgh, Scout camps, repairing boats and sailing have been replaced by trips with the church youth to Soul Survivor in Watford, Robbie driving the minibus, regular jaunts with the youth to Costa[4] and film days in the school holidays with the teenagers.

I worry about Robbie driving the minibus, being responsible for the safety of all those people, and I am always telling him to go carefully. And he does. I worry about idiots on the road, and I am always telling him to watch out for them. And he does that too. But, ultimately, tragically, there is nothing he can do.

Robbie's cousin Ellie-Jo is staying.

'Why don't you come along with me to Soul Survivor?' Robbie asks her on Saturday morning...

Ellie-Jo is back, sitting with me having a drink on the sofa. 'They're all a bit crazy,' she jokes, 'all larking around, having fun. The service was amazing, great music. Packed! Robbie went up the front to pray with people during the service. Then he took everyone to Pizza Hut on the way back. Sorry, Aunty Lizzie, I forgot to say, I don't need any tea.'

Next day, Ellie goes with Robbie to his church and to baptisms in the afternoon. I phone him with the news that her dad has gone into the hospice and that she will need a big hug. And in the next few weeks, whilst I am down in Cornwall on and off with Ellie, my sister and the rest of the family, I know (because Ellie tells me) that Robbie is texting her and supporting her and sending comforting messages.

'Hi, Mum!'

'Oh, hi, Robs. In the kitchen,' I call out.

He pushes open the door. 'Jus' come to abuse your internet for a while.'

'Tea?'

'Yeah, thanks. But in about an hour? Jus' round next door. But then I'll be back to Skype Ellie. Tea be good then!'

---

[4] Having to go through Robbie's finances after his accident has revealed just how much of his salary he spent entertaining the young people.

And he is off, with a quick toilet stop first, round next door where he is giving the neighbours' children some extra coaching sessions for their exams.

I am used to him popping in and out, the great advantage of having him fully absorbed in his own life but only a few minutes' drive away. The tea is all ready when he returns up the driveway, to sustain him through his Skype call with his cousin, setting her straight on some of the chemistry questions she is struggling with for her A level. They have already had several sessions together in this way, her in Cornwall, him in Reading. It is simply a continuation for him of the many times he has helped his younger siblings in the past. Not just in an academic capacity either.

I think of a photo that I haven't brought: Robbie, Tabby and Millie in the garage varnishing the coffee table. The girls are swamped in old T-shirts of Robbie's bearing slogans of heavy metal bands. They are quite young and Robbie is clearly supervising the operation. But they had fun. And we had an ultra-shiny table coated in yacht's varnish...

Now the counsellor is laughing as she looks at another picture. 'What a great moustache! What fun!'

For the last few years Robbie has been supporting Movember, growing facial hair and raising money. It is a great way for him to do something for charity because since his late teens, he has been a huge fan of facial hair in all its various forms: stubble, full beard, goatee, moustache.

'Robbie, are you trying to look like that or have you only shaved half your face?' Jack asks at tea one evening.

Robbie puts his hand up to feel. 'Oh, c**p, I've only done one half.'

But it has been a valid question of Jack's as some of the shaving jobs have been very creative.

His life is changing. He is a man; twenty-six, after all. He has matured. For the first time in twenty-three years, there is no Lego for Christmas! I think back to when he was a teenager and how narrowminded he was about his taste in music, how he wouldn't believe Nigey that he could ever like anything other than heavy metal. But now he has opened his mind to all sorts of things.

He talks to me about his conversations with the Catholic priest at school and I think how well that balances the more evangelical attitudes of the church he attends. Soon he will be moving out of his rented place as he prepares to be a married man. He has outgrown the sofa made from the leather back seats of his old Granada, and even purchased a new hall unit from Oak Furniture Land.

And after so many years spent sailing and scouting, his Friday evenings have become consumed with a new community youth group at the local leisure centre.

In just a few weeks' time he is due to get married...

‘Bye, love. See you soon,’ I call out as he prepares to leave.

The door shuts behind him. I hold my breath and wait for the doorbell, wait to retrieve for him whatever he’s forgotten.

But not this time.

This time he hasn’t forgotten anything.

Session 9

Reflections

The counsellor doesn't ask about God, how I feel as a Christian to lose my son. But it is something I need to talk about. I need to try and understand why God has let this happen; why God has allowed Robbie's life to end on earth when he was doing so much good for God down here; why he has been there for Robbie all the other times, through the operations, the biopsies, the scrapes on the bike and so many more occasions. Why now, when my close family is still reeling after my brother-in-law's death seven months ago?

I have so many questions and now I need some answers.

'You see,' I tell the counsellor, 'there were so many times when I can look back and see God's saving hand on Robbie's life. Not just the times I have told you about, but lots more.'

> *So here we are,* I think, *leaning back against the pillow and mulling over the events of the day.* Another traumatic incident, another occasion where Robbie can say, 'There, but for the grace of God, go I.' And he is not quite six.
>
> I can't quite take in what Tim Cocks is saying. I hardly know him but his son Thomas is in Robbie's year at school. He has brought Robbie back for me from John's sixth birthday party. It has been a 'swimming do' held at the school where John's dad is a teacher and house master. Robbie has been swimming there before and he is a very proficient swimmer for his age; very confident both on and under the water. So how can this have happened? How can Tim have needed to dive in and save my son?
>
> I think back carefully over Tim's words, the reality, the shock of what might have been slowly sinking in.

'Liz, no need for alarm, but I just want to mention that there was a bit of an incident at the pool.'

Tim had, he explained, been asked to act as a lifeguard, as there were no official ones on duty. But he was fully clothed sitting on the bench at the poolside, obviously expecting a noisy, boisterous afternoon and a headache rather than what actually happened. There had been large floats, he explained, and lots of children; lots of clambering onto the floats, clinging onto the side, games, shouting, screams. He watched as one particular float housing several shrieking boys capsized under their weight. And watched as they bobbed back up from under the water and clambered aloft again. And watched as the heaviness of their bodies pushed the float down under the water. Suddenly, he sprang up and dived, fully clothed with shoes still on, into the pool. Robbie had become trapped under the groaning weight of the float.

'Yes, I can understand what you are getting at,' the counsellor says.

'Was the timing of the traffic accident purely a case of being in the wrong place at the wrong time? Just a few seconds' delay and it would all have been so different.'

The counsellor nods in acknowledgement.

'But what about God? Where does he stand in all this?' I ask her now. I think how I have wrestled with this question; think how desperately I am searching for an answer. 'The Bible states in a few places that God has already set out the number of days we shall live, has already decided what length our life shall be, and that we can't change it.'

I scroll down my phone; search the Bible App. 'This is Job 14 verse 5,' I read out. 'A person's days are determined; you have decreed the number of his months and have set limits he cannot exceed.'

The counsellor watches me as I struggle to explain more fully.

'You see, if we all have an appointed time to die, what does that say about our free will? Does it really matter how we live our lives in terms of the risks we take, if it's already mapped out?' I pause. 'And what does that mean for Robbie? Was his life always going to end physically on that day in June? Were all the past scrapes and health scares irrelevant? Was this part of God's plan?'

The counsellor gives me a quizzical look. 'Well, I guess, none of us know.'

'It's so hard to look back at that horrendous week now with the knowledge that I didn't have then: when I prayed in all faith to God, as I always did, to keep Robbie safe – and I always made special reference to his journey to school – that God *knew*. He knew what that day would hold.' I brush away an escaping tear, fiddle with the tissue in my hand. 'But on another level, it's actually a comfort to me. It's reassuring to think that God had planned ahead; that he'd kept Robbie safe, just as I'd prayed, only not in the way that I'd envisaged; that the day and time were known so that Jesus could be ready and waiting with outstretched arms; that Robbie's room was prepared; that he was expected.'

The sun is streaming in, filtering through the half-open blinds and making patterns across the photos scattered on the table. I lean forwards, rummaging through them.

'The thing is,' I say looking up, 'Robbie would've been much safer that day if he'd been in his Land Rover and not on the motorbike.' I hand over a picture – of Robbie flat on his back on the drive, the Land Rover towering above him, sturdy, strong, dependable, as he tinkers with some tools under the vehicle itself. 'The bike'd been up for sale for months. Robbie was hoping that with the warmer weather he'd be able to shift it. But that week he did ride to school – the *first week* he'd taken his bike in months.'

'So Robbie hadn't been using the motorbike until that week,' the counsellor repeats.

It's so hard to say the next bit. 'Did God somehow *engineer it* that Robbie would go on the motorbike that day? Was that part of his plan? Or was Robbie simply exercising his free will and making his own choice?' I pause. 'But God already knew the consequence…'

'These are very difficult things. Valid questions,' the counsellor tells me, 'and there are no easy answers.'

'I've been reading so many books. Reading and reading. Trying to make sense of something that seems completely senseless.' I look out of the window, through the blinds, over the treetops, at a world that is confusing and painful. 'There was an elderly man, recently widowed, who spoke in church a few weeks ago. He mentioned a book by Timothy

Keller, *Walking with God Through Pain and Suffering*[5]. So I bought it and read it.'

'And how did you find that?'

'Yes, helpful.' I think about the big hardback book I have waded through; think about some of the arguments that it raises. 'You see, Keller addresses this issue of free will against predestination. He argues that God is ultimately in control of everything. His will always triumphs. So, a case of predestination. But he also says that God works his will in a way that still allows us to make choices and be fully accountable for the consequences of our actions. So, free will. Difficult to see how they can both work together.'

'Uh-huh.'

'Basically, it seems that everything's part of God's plan. But that plan works by using the choices we make, not by God making the choices for us.'

The counsellor nods but is silent, so I ask again, 'But how can that work?'

'These are very complex issues.' The counsellor sits back in her chair and waits for me to go on.

'I try and think of it like this,' I say, thinking about my simplistic explanation and wondering if it's right. 'When it's raining and I don't want to walk to work and get wet, I can plan to get a lift from Nigey. Nigey always chooses to take his car to work although he could walk too. So I already know his choice. By incorporating this into my plan, I'm not forcing Nigey to take his car. It's his decision. And it also means I can stay dry. So you see, it's a win-win for both of us. We both do what we want and both get the result we want.'

The counsellor smiles, 'Ah, yes! Very handy!'

'Thing is, I know God wants us to be free to worship him – to *choose* him rather than be programmed to.' I think about that billiard ball keyring from the arcade – how it only meant so much because Robbie himself had chosen to win it for me. I hadn't instructed him to spend his morning in that way. Like with any gift. 'There's this other book I've been reading too about free will, by Rauser.[6] It's all about God allowing

---

[5] *Walking with God Through Pain and Suffering;* Timothy Keller.
[6] *Finding God in the Shack;* Randal Rauser.

evil in the world so we have a choice between good and evil. So that if we opt for good, it becomes meaningful. A moral choice.'

The counsellor nods.

'But God already knows what choice we'll make. That's where it gets so confusing.'

The counsellor briefly shifts her gaze to the clock. She's a good listener and I know I've gone off track but it's a really important issue for me. I need so desperately to get some level of understanding as to why Robbie's accident happened at all and why it happened on that particular day. And how much of it had to do with Robbie's choices and those of the car driver, and how much to do with God.

'I've been looking at the Bible to try and see how God works this,' I tell the counsellor. 'So in the Old Testament there's a lot about the Israelites turning away from God. Despite his warnings of the devastation that'll follow, they do turn away. At the same time there's the Assyrians lusting after power and dominance.' I think how relevant this is still today, how this sort of thing is still happening. 'Anyway, the Assyrians attack – so that's their choice – war and destruction. The Israelites are defeated – so that's theirs, of turning away from God. Both have chosen their own path. But both, without realising it, are being used as part of God's plan.'

I glance over and catch the counsellor's eye; check she is still with me in this.

'And right at the very beginning, there's Adam and Eve. God gives Adam and Eve a choice. They're told not to eat the forbidden fruit but he doesn't make it impossible for them to eat it.'

I glance at the counsellor again and she nods briefly.

'So Adam and Eve eat from the tree. And the consequence is death entering the world. But what's so hard to deal with is that if God already knew what they would choose, does that mean that bringing sin into the world was part of his plan? I'm no theologian,' I smile, 'but I guess it's a no! It wasn't what God wanted. But he knew it'd happen. He'd already got it covered.'

I get out my mobile again and search for a passage.

'You see, God had planned that Jesus would be crucified and take on our sin from the very beginning. It says…' I look down at the screen and read out, '"God chose him as your ransom long before the world began, but now in these last days he has been revealed for your sake."'[7]

'I can see how much you've looked into this, how important it is to you,' the counsellor says.

I am at home. Upstairs. Sitting at the desk that we have now put in Robbie's old bedroom, the room at the front with the view over the street. The windows still have his old blue guitar curtains hanging either side. When Robbie first moved out it became a spare bedroom. But now we have rearranged things again, and as well as the desk that was at one time Robbie's, there are now lots of his things in here again: books, DVDs, instruments, amps, all here from his rented place. I have no idea what to do with them all. So I do nothing – just leave them scattered around me as I sit here at the desk. I am thinking about Judas, the disciple who betrayed Jesus; thinking about the part he played in God's plan;[8] thinking about whether he had any choice in his role or if he was a necessary casualty to bring God's plan to fruition. Surely God wouldn't be so unfair to Judas? But if he was, does that mean that others could fall by the wayside in the same way, their fate sealed for the sake of God's redemption of the world? The Bible before me is open. Jesus' own words, praying before his arrest, catch my eye: 'None has been lost except the one doomed to destruction so that Scripture would be fulfilled.'[9]

'So what about Judas?' I ask the counsellor now. 'Did he have any choice? We had a speaker at church a while back. Very dynamic. Very inspiring. He did a little plug for his latest book at the end. So of course, me being me, I bought it! *Paradoxology*[10] by Krish Kandiah. It tackles a lot of those puzzling questions which the Bible raises. He offers some really useful suggestions. But he also says that so much about God is a mystery because we aren't meant to understand everything. Not exactly the satisfactory answer I'd like. But I do get his point that faith often requires holding together seemingly irreconcilable concepts, trusting that

[7] 1 Peter 1:20 (NLT).
[8] See Acts 2:23.
[9] John 17:12.
[10] *Paradoxology;* Krish Kandiah.

God is in control. And he does know what he's doing. I guess we can't know everything or we'd be the same as God.'

Time is ticking on.

'It's a muddled picture,' I think out loud. 'It seems that Judas' choice has been made for him, doesn't it? It's like in Exodus and the story of God rescuing the Israelites from Pharaoh. Because he refuses to let them go, God is able to perform many miracles to save them, like sending all those plagues and the parting of the Red Sea. But there are some passages which say that God hardened Pharaoh's heart. And in Romans, in the New Testament, there's a part that says God can and does harden some hearts, and he can and does show mercy on some and not on others, and it's not for us to question.[11]'

The counsellor is frowning, studying my face.

'I hope I'm making sense,' I plough on, trying to express things more clearly. 'If you do a Google search, all sorts of commentaries and stuff come up about this. Best one for me is that we harden our own hearts by not yielding to God's will, not following what God wants but doing our own thing. But when we feel that God isn't doing what we want, when God doesn't yield to us, well, that's what it means by God hardening our hearts.'

'So does that help you when you think about Pharaoh and Judas?' the counsellor enquires.

'Yes, I think so. I mean, obviously I don't know for sure, but maybe Judas and Pharaoh both wanted God to do something else, something on their terms. Do things their way. So when he didn't, he was hardening their hearts.' I think about how things have been in my life and the decisions I've made. 'So on that basis, I have a choice now. God hasn't exactly done what I wanted. Robbie wasn't kept safe in the way that I prayed. So I could let that harden my heart; I could let *God* harden my heart.'

It's my decision but God already knows what I'll choose. I'm getting tangled up in my own arguments.

'I still don't have a satisfactory explanation of why the car driver was on Robbie's side of the road that morning,' I tell the counsellor, my mind back now to the start of our session. 'All the conditions were perfect, great visibility, clear road markings, no one was speeding, no alcohol or

---

[11] See Romans 9:16-21.

drugs had been taken, no phone was being used, nothing ran across the road, the car was small, the road was familiar. Robbie had all the correct safety gear. The police told us that the ambulance staff commented on how well protected Robbie was – as usual, he was wearing his back protector. Both vehicles were in good condition too – Robbie's motorbike had its MOT the week before.'

The counsellor says to me, 'Yes, it sounds like all should have been OK.'

'We were given an eleventh-hour confession, just before sentencing, from the car driver that he was looking down at the speedometer and, when he looked up, found himself on the wrong side of the road. I find this impossible to believe. If this were the case, there'd be continual accidents! We all have to glance down to check our speed! But because he was on his own in the car, there were no close witnesses and he refused to talk to the police (his right, apparently), no one'll ever really know.'

I am surprised how angry I still sound when I say these things out loud.

'And so, despite every piece of evidence showing the car driver was on Robbie's side of the road, the police couldn't charge him with dangerous driving. That vital missing piece meant there was no proof of why he was on the wrong side, what caused it.' Then I add, 'But what I do know is that despite a stipulation on his driving licence, the car driver *wasn't wearing his glasses.'*

'And how does that make you feel?'

'Angry... Confused... Oh, I don't know. I just can't see how that would've meant the car ended up on the wrong side of the road. I mean, he'd managed to drive to that point OK.'

The counsellor is shifting in her chair, leaning forwards. She's evidently getting ready to close the session.

'Who knows the impact?' I shrug. 'But it was obviously a wilful choice by the car driver not to wear them.'

So, I think, on that day in June, Robbie was exercising his free will to ride a motorbike and the car driver was exercising his not to wear glasses. And we all know the consequence. Was God using the car driver as part of his purpose and part of his plan? I don't know. All I can do is give all these worries to God – and try to trust in him.

'Rauser, that guy I mentioned earlier who writes about free will, well, he says that God doesn't give clear reasons for allowing specific evils as it wouldn't be helpful for us to know. It's best the details of why we suffer are known only to God.' I think about this. 'He says only God knows the whole picture. Only God knows the end from the beginning. Only God knows the impact of every event on every person; the ripple effect of every single thing.'

As I leave the counsellor and walk to the car, I ponder on the fact that only God knows how many people have been, and will be, influenced by the life of my elder son, both in this life and beyond it; and that one day, when I am with Robbie again in our eternal home, I will have all the answers.[12]

---

[12] See 1 Corinthians 13:12.

I'm in the kitchen clearing up when the doorbell rings. Someone is charging down the stairs calling, 'I'll get it!'

My heart is thumping. I'm holding my breath. 'Who is it?' I call. Hoping. Longing. Yearning.

'Amazon.'

My face falls, my arms drop, my heart sinks.

Not Robbie then. Not Robbie again.

SESSION 10

Reasoning

The counsellor also wants to spend time looking at the other losses I have faced.

'My first contact with death was when I was quite young,' I tell her, 'and my godmother died. I hadn't seen her often but was given a photo of her to keep. I remember wrapping the picture in cotton wool and shutting it in a drawer – I didn't know if I was OK to have it on display.'

Now that I am reminded of that picture, I wonder where it is. In this sea of photographs that I've brought with me, I know for certain that there isn't one of her.

'And when I was thirteen, I saw a lady commit suicide in front of a tube train.' I think about how I had to sleep with the light on for months afterwards; how now, thirty-six years later, her image still remains with me.

'That must have been so hard.'

I want to shout out to the counsellor that it's OK, I'm pretty well acquainted with pain, heartache and suffering, thank you; that I already felt like I'd had my share of misery; that it was completely unfair that I had to lose Robbie too.

But I don't raise my voice. It's not the counsellor's fault. Instead I try to be matter-of-fact. 'In the space of just seven years my sister had a brain haemorrhage and strokes at the age of forty-two, my dad was diagnosed with prostate cancer that's spread to his bones and kidney nodes, my mum had a minor stroke, my father-in-law died from lung cancer with my mother-in-law dying three months afterwards from lymphoma meningitis, my brother-in-law died at the age of almost forty-nine after a two-year battle with a brain tumour and my elder son had major bowel surgery, was diagnosed with Barrett's oesophagus and had his life taken by a car driver on the wrong side of the road...'

But it's no good. My voice betrays me. I am angry. I am distraught. My heart is beating so fast the counsellor must surely be able to hear.

'It's ridiculous, but I feel an affinity to Job,' I say, shaking my head and thinking about the Old Testament story. 'Poor Job! – whose house and cattle are destroyed, children are killed and who is afflicted with terrible boils; a man whose life is devastated by sorrow and pain; a righteous, devout man. He'd been blessed and his life was going well.'

The counsellor is watching me as I struggle to compose myself.

'I guess his challenge, and mine, is to be faithful and continue to trust in God when life isn't going well and "bad things" happen. Job has a lot of questions, a lot of things he needs to ask God. Just like I do. How can suffering feature in God's plan?'

'I hear what you're saying. You've been dealt so many blows, so many losses; and you're wondering where God is in all this pain...'

'Yes, that's it. Where *is* God in all this pain? Going back to the Bible, I think books like Job are important. They're there for a reason. It's like that old Sunday school rhyme, you know? "God hasn't promised skies always blue, but strength for the journey all the way through." God never says it'll be easy. Or a smooth ride. Job questions God about why all these terrible things have happened, but he isn't given any kind of explanation.'

I pause, remembering other places in the Bible where there is suffering, but unlike in Job, healing *does* happen. Such as the blind man in John's Gospel. Jesus says that the man's sight is restored so that the wonder of God can be revealed in him.[13] And in the story of Lazarus a bit further on, Jesus raises Lazarus from the dead so that through the suffering of Lazarus and his family, God can reveal his power and many come to believe in him.[14]

Now I tell the counsellor, 'God doesn't even give Job a reassurance that his suffering will be used to reveal God's glory. Or so he can better reach out and comfort others.' Job is such a difficult book to plough through. But it's definitely worth the effort. 'Job's reminded that God is the one who's in charge of everything. Nothing came into being without him. As God is the creator of the universe, it's totally up to him what he

---

[13] John 9:1.
[14] John 11:4.

chooses to do with it all. God is omniscient. He knows everything about everything.'

The counsellor nods.

'So that includes why the "bad things" happen. I guess, as humans, this knowledge totally exceeds our comprehension. I mean, we don't really understand other people, so we're hardly going to understand God!'

'Of course.'

'It won't surprise you that I've been reading a book about this!' I smile at the counsellor and she smiles back, nodding. 'Actually, Nigey bought this one but I've read it too. It's by Harold Kushner – *When Bad Things Happen to Good People*[15]. Very apt title. Kushner addresses the question of why God "allows" bad things to happen when it's totally within his power to stop them. I mean, he could intervene, perform a miracle. Or stop the bad thing happening in the first place.' I pause. 'And sometimes he does.'

'Yes, that's true,' the counsellor agrees.

'Much of Kushner's book is based on Job. He has three possible statements that he uses to address the problem of Job's suffering.' I count them out on my fingers. 'So (a) God is in control, has power over all, his will triumphs. Then (b) God is impartial, upright, fair and dishes out to people what they deserve, rewarding the good and punishing the bad. And (c) the understanding that Job's a good man.' I pause. 'Hopefully I can put this in a way that makes sense. But basically, Kushner argues that if God is just and powerful, which is (a) and (b), then Job must be a sinner who deserves what's happened to him. But we're told that Job's a good man (c). So, if Job's a good man (c) and God causes all that happens to him (a), then God can't be just. But we know that God is just (b). So, if bad things are happening to Job and he deserves better (c) and (b), then God can't be all powerful. But we know that God is sovereign over all (a).'

'Yes. I think I just about follow that,' the counsellor smiles. 'A bit of a conundrum!'

I smile back. 'Kushner says that Job's friends who're trying to comfort him reconcile the arguments by believing that Job isn't a good man. God's

---

[15] *When Bad Things Happen to Good People;* Harold S. Kushner.

all powerful and God's just, so Job must actually deserve the bad things that are happening. Seems a bit harsh!'

I think of all the people who've tried to comfort me, and I can't believe that any of them would even begin to contemplate that we deserved to lose Robbie.

'Kushner's conclusion,' I say, returning my thoughts to the book, 'as I understand it, is that Job is good and God is just but he isn't all powerful (a). Some things are beyond his control. Kushner believes that the universe is still in a process of creation; within this turmoil, there are some things that God can't control.' I take a deep breath and look up at the counsellor. 'I don't agree. I believe that God is omnipotent. Nothing's impossible for him. Kandiah, that guy I mentioned in our last session, believes that Job is confirmation that God's in control of everything. At the start of Job, Satan goes before God and asks his permission to send misfortune on Job. Kandiah says, this fact in a book about suffering confirms that God has power over everything. Even suffering.'

'That's an interesting point,' the counsellor offers, shifting in her chair and crossing her legs.

'Have you read William Young's *The Shack*[16]?' I ask her.

She shakes her head. 'No. I've heard of it but never read it myself.'

'The basic storyline is that Mack's daughter Missy gets taken from a campsite by a serial killer and although her body isn't found, her bloodied dress is discovered in the shack. A few years afterwards, Mack receives a letter telling him to go to the shack, and there he meets God, Jesus and the Holy Spirit. It's a bit of a Marmite kind of book – people seem to love it or hate it. Personally, I think it's a good read. Overall, an uplifting, inspiring message based on Christianity.'

The counsellor nods.

'I know the actual theology of the book has been questioned by some people – but it's a novel, after all. Still, some theologians have sought to explain the book from biblical truths.'

The counsellor nods again.

'Like Rauser. He argues that God allows evil and evil events to occur because he'll use them for greater good. So in "The Shack", through Missy's death, Mack's drawn closer to God and his life's transformed. Rauser uses this to illustrate God using evil for good.' I sit forwards in

---

[16] *The Shack;* William Young.

my chair and uncross my legs. 'And whilst I do agree that God can, and sometimes does, use suffering to bring glory, I don't agree that a loving God would allow hundreds of people to suffer horrific deaths and torture every day just for the greater good of humankind.' It's an appalling thought. But then, I've no idea why horrendous things happen to God's people. Or why only some prayers are answered and God intervenes. Or why some really corrupt people seem to have everything.

'The problem of suffering is an age-old dilemma that many people have struggled with.'

'It's so hard to accept that it doesn't have a neat, easily understood answer.' I think of the 'magic cream' that the nurses gave Robbie that 'First Terrible Time'; how difficult it was to explain that the nurses were trying to make him better. The pain of the injection, the insertion of the cannula, were necessary for his operation, his healing. Robbie couldn't understand; he was only four. He had to trust me, trust the medical staff. Without answers to my questions, I guess in the same way I'll have to dig deep in faith that God will reveal to me what I need to know and keep hidden what I don't.

> I am sitting up in bed. I am calmer now. I can see that Nigey, exhausted, has gone back to sleep. I can hear his slow, gentle, rhythmic breathing. The sudden gripping pain in the right side of my back that had spread round to my chest has eased. The pain, travelling up to my mouth, my teeth, my ears, my head, the sharp burning in my heart, has subsided. But still that *other* pain is here; the pain that seers through my body, that grabs my insides, rippling them violently apart. Again. *Again and again.* The ache that is lodged in my breast bone. The agony that won't go away.

'When I think of the constant pain and heartache of losing Robbie, to voluntarily give up your son in the way that God gave up Jesus is difficult to grasp.'

The counsellor is having a sip of water. She looks up and acknowledges what I've said.

'I can't even begin to imagine the sacrifice he made for us, allowing those wicked things to happen to his only son. And to think he didn't just do this for "good people" but allowed Jesus to be tortured and go to hell for everyone. *For absolutely everyone.* God suffered. Jesus suffered,' I continue. 'Jesus was misunderstood, abused, rejected – even by his friends – taunted, physically tortured and killed. And on top of all that, when his need was greatest, he was cut off from God; went to hell, literally, for us.'

The counsellor gives a reassuring nod and gazes at me kindly.

'I understand that Adam and Eve ate the forbidden fruit, bringing evil into the world, and with it sin and death. And I know that there's evil in all of us. So for God to defeat evil but not destroy us at the same time, he chose to conquer the consequence of evil, which is death. And the only way to do that was to sacrifice Jesus, the one without sin, to allow him to take on all our sin and to die in our place. Totally amazing!' A powerful image of the cross comes into my head, a picture by Charlie Mackesy,[17] that speaks so much to me. 'So on the day God chooses to defeat sin once and for all, he'll be able to wipe out the remainder of the human race, as all who believe in him will be saved through the blood of Jesus.'

The counsellor, giving a brief nod in acknowledgment, is shifting in her chair, probably wondering where all this is going.

'It's scary facing the reality of Satan,' I say simply, 'to acknowledge the presence of evil, to recognise the power that it holds in this world and beyond.' I reach over, pick up my phone and scroll down the Bible App. 'This is what it says in Ephesians: "For our struggle is not against flesh and blood, but against the rulers, against the authorities, against the powers of this dark world and against the spiritual forces of evil in the heavenly realms."[18]'

'That's powerful reading. How does that make you feel in relation to what happened to Robbie?'

'That there's some huge conflict, some gigantic battle going on out there; something frightening that I can't even get my head around. I feel that losing Robbie, that our suffering, is somehow caught up in all this; that our lives are just a miniscule part of an eternal plan.'

The counsellor is watching me, waiting.

---

[17] The picture can be viewed online at: *http://charliemackesy.com/paintings/img_8190*

[18] Ephesians 6:12.

'Adrian Plass has looked at the issue of Satan.[19] He mentions several Bible passages which point to a universe where there's war in heaven, Satan's hurled like lightning banished to the earth, and sinning angels are exiled to hell, chained in darkness, awaiting judgement. Plass argues that this spiritual warfare's a continuing reality.' I look up. 'That means it's happening right here, right now. He says it's the cosmic picture that's in play; that we need to think of suffering against this backdrop. A spiritual war. Good against evil.'

'Hmm... so, intense supernatural events,' the counsellor ponders.

'Yes. Like I said, *powerful, scary.* And real. But ultimately God will be victorious.'

A gust of wind is blowing the blind, disturbing my photos piled on the table. I look across and my attention is drawn by a couple of small girls all ready for bed.

'This a picture of me and my sister in shop-bought nighties!' I hand the photo to the counsellor. 'We usually had homemade ones, so bought nighties were a real treat!' My sister, two years my senior, towers over my head in the photo; not so any more. She has an enormous grin on her face. 'D'you remember the test card that used to be on telly years ago when there were no programmes on? The girl with long hair?'

The counsellor smiles and nods.

'I used to think it was my sister!'

I tell the counsellor about the miraculous healing of my sister from her brain haemorrhage. How I was there when she came round after five hours of open brain surgery. How every hour she was questioned: how many children do you have; when is your birthday; what year is it? And how she didn't know those things. But over time, and with a lot of prayers, she has battled to regain a lot of her speech, to learn how to ride a bike again, to co-ordinate both sides of her body.

I tell the counsellor about the miraculous healing of my dad; that although he is still ill, the doctors initially didn't think he would live beyond the next few weeks. And now it is five-and-a-half years later.

'Since June 13th, 2014, my attention has been drawn more and more to the miraculous stories throughout the Bible, both in the Old and New Testament, about God restoring people's lives and bringing people back from the dead,' I say to the counsellor now. 'And I think about that day

---

[19] *Blind Spots in the Bible;* Adrian Plass.

when we had the horrific news and I wonder why God didn't choose to raise Robbie from the dead?'

I pause. The room is still. The counsellor is still. There is the slightest murmur of seconds ticking away from the clock on the table. Otherwise all is silent. My mind has returned to that horrendous day.

'I never asked him to.' My voice is small and hollow in the still room. 'I never prayed that God would revive Robbie. Certainly not initially. Not on that day. My prayers were more desperate than hopeful. I pleaded with God that it wasn't Robbie. I prayed that it wasn't true, that it couldn't have happened, that it was mistaken identity and that it was all part of a horrendous nightmare that would stop and I would see him again.'

I want the counsellor to say something. I want her to tell me that it wasn't because my prayers were too late; that it wasn't because I didn't pray hard enough. But she folds her hands in her lap and says nothing.

'So you see, it's another question that troubles me. Why does God heal some and not others? What was special about the people in the Bible who had their lives restored?' I think of the many books and articles I have read about this. One thing that seems certain is that it had nothing to do with whether they were strong in their faith or not. 'There are many examples where Jesus heals non-believers and other instances where those faithful to him aren't healed. The apostle Paul prays three times to be cured but isn't.'

The counsellor nods.

'Another conclusion,' I continue, trying to answer my own question, 'is that God used those miracles, as he does with other cases of healing, for a greater purpose. In the New Testament John refers to Jesus' miracles as signs – signposts to who Jesus was.' Then I remember that it was only after Elijah revived her son that the widow believed that Elijah was from God and spoke the truth.[20] The miracle was a way to affirm God – a demonstration of his power and truth. So, I realise that the same principle applies in the Old Testament too.

'It's occurred to me, though, that where people are raised to life, it means their life is restored. So they're back in their old life. If this had happened to Robbie, from my own selfish point of view, I can't describe the joy and elation I'd be feeling. But Robbie would be back living with

---

[20] 1 Kings 17.

the Barrett's oesophagus that may have led to oesophageal cancer, back living with the health problems of a troublesome bowel and scar tissue, back living with all the old stresses and strains of everyday life with all its anxieties. And there'd still have to come a day when he'd die.'

The counsellor nods in agreement.

'Sometimes when I've been reading, it's like a light switching on. Words jump out at me and suddenly things start to make sense. Like when I recently read Jack Wellman's online article.[21] It challenged my understanding of healing miracles. He argues that surely the greatest miracle that God can perform is to change what's in someone's heart, to open their mind to God's love, to call them into his presence. By doing this, God's performing a miracle that won't just restore an old life, that won't just bodily resuscitate them, that isn't just a temporary healing; but a miracle that'll result in eternal life, a miracle that's everlasting.'

'So how does that make you feel in regard to Robbie?' the counsellor wants to know.

'Well, obviously, restoring Robbie's human life hasn't been part of God's plan. But Robbie has received this eternal miracle of new life from God. He's been wholly healed. He's living a new life where, as it says in Revelation, "[God] will wipe every tear from their eyes. There will be no more death, or mourning or crying or pain."[22]'

It's something very positive to take away from my session.

---

[21] *https://www.whatchristianswanttoknow.com/does-god-still-work-miracles-today*

[22] Revelation 21:4.

I'm in the kitchen clearing up when my mobile beeps. Someone is calling down the stairs, 'That was your phone!'

My heart is thumping. I'm holding my breath. I open the message. Hoping. Longing. Yearning.

Just the dentist. Appointment reminder.

My face falls, my arms drop, my heart sinks.

Not Robbie then. Not Robbie again.

SESSION 11

Renaissance

'Of course, Robbie was a Christian, had a strong faith, and that does give me an amazing comfort. He'd already committed his life to Jesus.' I rummage through the things I've brought with me. 'This is what Jane wrote to me. She was one of the leaders of Upper Room. That's the church group Robbie was part of as a teenager.'

I read out to the counsellor the little card that Jane has sent me: 'I always looked forward to him being there (Upper Room) as he always asked so many challenging questions. It made for a very lively Upper Room session with few awkward silences and plenty of discussion! He was one of the first older members of Upper Room we encouraged to lead the younger ones in a discussion group. And, of course, it was at his very forthright instigation Upper Room started running the Traidcraft stall two Sundays a month.'

'Yes, I remember that story you told me about the Traidcraft stall.' The counsellor smiles, sitting back in her chair.

'Robbie was Christened when he was just nine weeks old,' I continue, putting down Jane's card and lifting up a photograph instead. 'He wore the family Christening gown and a pair of tights – poor Robbie! Look! He's so perfect. So gorgeous. Lying in my arms wearing the beautiful lace gown. It was important for me to dedicate his life to God.'

I take the picture from the counsellor and lay it back on the table with the others.

'A very special moment,' she says gently.

'I read this article about a young lady, about Robbie's age, who died in a car crash on her way to Bible college. The writer said that although Mary died young, her death wasn't untimely as she was prepared and ready to die. *But what does that mean?* I can see that if you're suffering from a terminal illness, you may have thought about death more than maybe someone who isn't. But Mary was young and surely not expecting her life would end soon.' I think about this question in relation to Robbie too. 'The article argues that as Mary had already given her life to Jesus and had been obedient to his calling by going to Bible College, she'd put all her preparations in place. So she was ready.'

'Yes,' the counsellor replies. 'So how do feel about that from Robbie's point of view?'

'Well, from birth he was brought up as a Christian – as a member of a church congregation. But it wasn't until he was a teenager that he came to faith for himself.' I think again about Upper Room. 'Staff at Farnborough Hill – that's the school where Robbie was teaching – told me that a few weeks before the "accident", Robbie had said to his pupils that he wasn't afraid to die; that when the time came he wanted to be able to stand before God knowing he'd lived his life to the full.'

'That's remarkable,' the counsellor says. 'How does that make you feel?'

'That he can certainly attest to that.' I pause. 'And it comforts me too. And reminds me that Robbie was never scared of anything.'

'How amazing!'

'And like Mary, Robbie's preparations were already in place; a committed member of his congregation at church, with all his Christian and other youth work, living out his calling to teach and with a future planned in which he intended to continue his ministry to God.'

I fish in my bag and hand the counsellor something to read. But before she starts, I tell her, 'This is what Farnborough Hill School wrote on their website: "We entrust Rob into the embrace of God who he loved so much. May he now see Him face to face."[23]'

I sit back in my chair and cross my ankles, waiting for the counsellor to read what I have just given her. 'It's what the senior pastors at the Network Vineyard Church wrote in the newspaper in tribute to Robbie. "It's hard to try and capture the essence and immeasurable value in a few words, of one such as Rob, and there are very many elements that stand out as great qualities and gifts which went together to comprise the person he was. He was a young man whose strong Christian faith led him to invest hugely in the lives of the youth both in the church and outside,

---

[23] *http://www.cisc.uk.net/index.php/home/news/115-farnborough-hill-teacher-dies-in-tragic-accident*

to whom he was both a wise mentor, and someone always ready to help in a wide range of practical ways. His kindness, patience and warmth brought encouragement, fun and steadiness to the lives of others, and he was both friend and role model to many. Rob's brilliant musical talent, particularly his drumming skills, were a wonderful asset to the worship ministry and, like so much else, will be greatly missed. For the many people who deeply loved, appreciated and valued Rob, his loss is so very painful, and will continue to be felt, alongside the residing memories of the wonderful young man he was."[24]'

'What wonderful words. How special he was.'

'How special he *is,*' I correct the counsellor. *And,* I think, *how special he will always be.*

'Robbie was in the middle of doing so many good things,' I tell her now. 'He was about to get married. He was building his future. He'd found a school where he was valued and could make a difference. He was supporting so many young people; involved in youth work in so many ways through clubs, music, sailing, teaching. God could've continued to work through Robbie using all his many gifts and talents. But he chose instead to continue Robbie's ministry through his death, not his life. It's so hard to understand why.'

The counsellor reads aloud some of the many wonderful messages that have been passed on to us about Robbie.

'"A touching tribute to Robbie's teaching abilities as all current A level students received A* grades today. Many congratulations to those girls and any others he taught receiving results today or next week. Mr Scho/Mr S is so very proud of you all."'[25]

'"Rob had a calling, a real vocation."'[26]

I smile. 'All those lovely messages from his pupils and their parents. It makes me think about the legacy that Robbie's left; about his change of career choice to teaching rather than to work for a Formula 1 team that he'd dreamt about. It wasn't a decision he took lightly. But it was what he felt God wanted him to do with his life.' I pause, thinking that his teaching, compassion and giving to others has left a much more

---

[24] *www.getreading.co.uk/news/local-news/talented-popular-science-teacher-greatly-7287594*

[25] From the Facebook tribute page.

[26] From the Farnborough Hill pastoral Head of Year 10.

memorable and God-given legacy than working for a Formula 1 team, developing a new component for an even faster racing car, would have done. 'Through his teaching, his compassion for others, his work with young people, his love, he can still reach out and touch us now,' I exclaim.

I pass the counsellor a beautiful poem written by one of Robbie's pupils at Farnborough Hill.

There are some people who are like rain
in the fact that they cover you
gently with their touch.
Sometimes, they can annoy you
or even stop you from doing something,
but deep down you know that you need them.
Rain makes the plants grow,
it provides water in times of drought,
it is made up of little bits of stardust.
Rain has such a big impact on so many people
in a selfless way
because each raindrop dies when it hits the ground
in order to help the rest of us.
Mr Schofield was our rain,
and we will remember him as such,
loved by all,
valued by all,
never forgotten.

'Those precious words remind me of this passage in Deuteronomy 32:2,' I say, reading out. '"Let my teaching fall like rain and my words descend like dew, like showers on new grass, like abundant rain on tender plants." And that bit in John about a kernel of wheat needing to fall to the ground and die in order to produce many seeds.[27]'

'Powerful images,' the counsellor concurs.

As I put the poem back in my bag, I see something else in there, something else I have brought to share with the counsellor.

---

[27] John 12:24.

I am surrounded by socks: pairs, singles, plain, patterned, worn, unworn, threadbare, thick; longer ones, shorter ones. So many socks! How can Robbie have had so many socks? I don't say *owned,* as some are definitely *borrowed.* Some are certainly Jack's; but all had their home with Robbie. He wore them all, regardless; matched or mismatched.

But not all the socks are as they were. I am making some into sock monkeys. It's a fact that surprises even me; sewing and I have never been the best of friends. Yet here I am, needle in hand, transforming a couple of socks into a monkey. And I am enjoying it; handling his socks; finding it pleasing to see the worn places where his toes rested, the darkened patches that nestled his heels; creating something new out of something that's old; making something to remember out of something forgotten; making something to keep out of something that's gone.

The counsellor holds the sock monkey, twisting it round, turning it over. 'It's exquisite! Beautiful! A wonderful keepsake.'

'Yes. Socks are such a symbol of Robbie. His trademark odd socks. And the monkeys have been a good thing to be able to give to others.'

I put the monkey down on the table.

'Robbie was in the middle of living,' I stress again.

The counsellor smiles and nods.

'His place was, of course, just as he had left it that morning: clothes on the floor, empty wrappers on his desk, dirty mugs, piles of paper, stacks of stuff. *Everywhere.* Waiting. Waiting for him to return. Expecting him to return.'

'That must have been so painful – seeing everything left just like that.'

'Yes. Heartbreaking. So difficult to accept. A life that was so unfinished. Your mind just doesn't believe they won't be back. All this time later, I still can't believe he won't be back.'

The counsellor murmurs something and nods.

'Apart from a few very prized possessions – guitars, drum kit, Land Rover and boat – oh, and his iPad and phone – he didn't much care for clobber; wasn't one for needing it all; didn't hanker after the newest models. His iPad had had a cracked screen for ages. There's that well-known verse in Matthew.' I recite from memory: '"Do not store up for yourselves treasures on earth, where moths and vermin destroy, and where thieves break in and steal. But store up for yourselves treasures in heaven, where moths and vermin do not destroy, and where thieves do not break in and steal. For where your treasure is, there your heart will be also."[28]'

'Uh-huh.'

'If you think about Paul, he wrote so much of the New Testament. I expect when he died, he left behind very few physical possessions. But that doesn't matter because his legacy is all his writings which we still read and study today. How enduring is that! And it's also a reminder that you don't have to know someone personally for their legacy to influence you. The challenge is to choose wisely what to invest in.'

'Yes.' The counsellor is nodding.

'When I think of Robbie, he didn't have any property or money to leave. But I pray that what will endure was his passion to educate and nurture the youth, his generosity of spirit, his kindness, his sense of fun. I heard it somewhere that Mother Teresa's stance was, what counts isn't what you do but the love that you put into it.[29]'

'That's a great thing to remember.'

'On the morning of June 13th, Robbie had a cake in the top box of his motorbike. He'd baked it the evening before for his pupils. It makes me think about how much he cared about those young people; how much they mattered to him.'

I stop, my mind on other ways to leave legacies.

'Robbie always carried a donor card in his wallet. A way to leave a legacy and give a life to someone else when yours has physically come to an end.'

'Yes,' the counsellor nods, 'that can be important for some people.'

'For Robbie, praise God, the move to the other side was so swift that organ donation wasn't a possibility. Or the gifting of anything else physically. Although, I admit, I do have mixed feelings about that.' These things are so hard to talk about. All I can do is speak in a detached way. An abstract way. My head can't contemplate the reality of what I'm saying. 'But it was Robbie's wish, so had it been viable, it would've been done.'

---

[28] Matthew 6:19-21.

[29] See, for example, *https://www.goodreads.com/quotes/664276-it-is-not-how-much-we-do-but-how-much*

'It's an extremely difficult, delicate issue.' The counsellor is sympathetic; trying to understand.

'The thing is that although I spoke to that policeman in Cyprus who implied there was a length of time between the accident and losing Robbie, Kelly told me afterwards that those were all official timings – that the loss of Robbie was instant. The official time recorded included all the attempts by the ambulance crew to revive him. So it was too late for organ donation.' I am back there, back in that villa, reliving the worst day of my life.

I struggle to focus my thoughts on the session. 'Organ donation wasn't something that we'd talked about much. But Robbie'd told me he was a registered donor. To be honest, it's something that I've never really liked to think about; never thought I would *have to* think about. But I do understand these things have to be done straightaway. Virtually my first phone call with Kelly in Cyprus was about organ donation. We were still in total shock – couldn't even take in there'd been an accident or believe what'd happened – and we were being asked about organ donation! Kelly talked to me about it again when we were in the taxi going to the airport – about donating some of his tissues. But that wasn't possible either.'

I think about what Nigey told me afterwards, too. He thought that Dick, the accident investigation officer, had said to him that as a post-mortem was needed, as it was a criminal case, there couldn't be organ donation.

'But I know that Robbie's spirit lives on in my life and the lives of many others. His life is still having a living impact.' I lean over and offer some cards to the counsellor. 'Here are just a few messages from the hundreds we've received.

'"Rob will be sadly missed but warmly remembered here at Farnborough Hill. He touched so many lives and I'm grateful I had the chance to know him, working alongside him. He always bought a smile to the department and was an inspiration to so many."[30]

'"May the bright light that is your lovely son Rob shine even more brightly in the years to come, in the hearts of all who loved him."[31]

---

[30] From a colleague.

[31] From parents of a pupil at Farnborough Hill.

'"We hear nothing but wonderful things about Robbie all the time – what a marvellous impression he made on so many people – my children included."[32]'

Now I check my phone. 'On December 24th last year, Jack posted onto Robbie's Facebook tribute page[33], "Happy 28th birthday, Robbie. 2015 has seen £9,000 raised in your name, a true testament to the remarkable legacy you have left."' I look up, meet the counsellor's eye. 'By giving generously, a staggering total of at least £30,000 has been raised in Robbie's memory for several different charities including Barrett's Oesophagus Campaign[34], Hope to Albania[35], Just Round the Corner[36], Vineyard youth minibus[37], Cruse[38] and Brake[39].'

'That's fantastic!'

'Yes. And money that would've been spent on Robbie's birthday and Christmas presents is now going to Centre Point to support a young person each year. Young people mattered so much to Robbie. The money's been raised in so many different ways, through giving sites, a calendar, sponsored swims, marathons, bike rides and charity social events, with more planned for the future. Robbie was all for having fun and it's good to be able to have fun, get together to support each other and raise money too. And I want to pay tribute to Jack, who's been such a driving force behind much of this fundraising, running events and encouraging others to do the same.'

There is just time for the counsellor to flick through some pictures taken at the Charity Ball: family, friends, teachers, pupils, those who've known him, those who haven't, Christians, non-Christians; all united for Robbie.

---

[32] From a mother of children from Vineyard youth.

[33] *www.facebook.com/robbieschofield.1987*

[34] The condition Robbie suffered from.

[35] Robbie took part in and attended various charity events.

[36] Christian youth work that Robbie worked alongside on the holiday play schemes.

[37] Robbie drove the minibus but it was in need of replacement

[38] Support for the bereaved.

[39] The road safety charity.

I'm walking to work when I see the bike.

Someone is riding down the street.

My heart is thumping. I'm holding my breath.

I watch. The motorbike nears. I check the face. Hoping. Longing. Yearning.

Just a bike. Just another biker.

My face falls, my arms drop, my heart sinks. Not Robbie then. Not Robbie again.

Session 12

Reassurance

'It's impossible,' I tell the counsellor, 'to convey the absolute shock, the total unexpectedness, the utter disbelief that hits you full on. From nowhere. How one second can be separated from the next by a vast, black, bottomless pit. How just that one second can literally shatter your whole world. And you are completely unprepared. There's no warning, nothing to make the second before seem any different from normal; yet in the next moment, your future is changed forever.'

The counsellor nods. 'It must have been a terrible shock.'

'Just seven months before, I'd spent time down in Cornwall with my sister as her husband was dying. It was harrowing; long, drawn out; very difficult to watch. We'd all known for a considerable time that he wouldn't get better. I'd already said my goodbyes to him at least twice, just in case. When the end came, it was a release for him, a relief to see he wasn't suffering any more. He was ready and so were we.'

The counsellor shifts in her chair as I continue.

'With Robbie it was totally the opposite. No one was expecting what happened. I was looking forward to seeing him when we got back from holiday. The end was so swift. I struggle so much with not having been there with him; not having had any time to have said goodbye; to have so many unsaid things that now there is no chance to say.'

I look at the counsellor as she nods and reflects back to me what I've told her. I wonder if she's ever experienced anything remotely similar. If not, how can she ever realise or comprehend the pain, the anguish, I carry around always about that unspoken goodbye; or how difficult I find it to hear about the stories of others who've lost but still had that last bit of time together? I must hang on in faith that there was no goodbye because it wasn't the end. We'll be together again. One day.

'Have you heard the story of the angel who appeared before a man and granted him one wish – anything that he desired?'

'Not sure. Go on,' the counsellor tells me.

'Well, the man, after thinking this through, requested to see the next day's newspaper. He imagined finding out which stocks had significantly increased in value from the day before, investing his money in them and making his fortune. But on being presented with tomorrow's newspaper, the man was shocked to discover, catching sight of the obituaries, that there was his name.'

'Be careful what you wish for, I guess.'

'Exactly. In the Bible it warns us that our time will come when we're not expecting it.' I turn to my trusty source, to my Bible App, and read out the well-known passage in Matthew 24. '"Therefore, keep watch, because you do not know on what day your Lord will come. But understand this: If the owner of the house had known at what time of night the thief was coming, he would have kept watch and would not have let his house be broken into. So you also must be ready, because the Son of Man will come at an hour when you do not expect him."'[40]

'We're so lucky,' I reflect out loud, 'living in an age where God's message is available freely, in so many different formats – hard copies, electronically, the Internet, texting, audio. And in the UK we can worship God openly.'

'Yes, of course,' the counsellor replies.

'The Christian message is still, I think, being taught to some extent to all school children in this country. I know that through organisations such as REInspired, more children are being reached. For Robbie and the others, attending a Church of England school meant assemblies had a Christian content. Some services were held in the church next door.' I cast my mind back to that Year 6 nativity held in the church, Robbie with his classmates decked out as angels. 'Sadly, I know this kind of exposure to Christianity has taken a back seat. But there are still plenty of ways we can access the Christian message.'

I shift in my chair and fiddle with my necklace.

'It's like in the Bible when God gives the Israelites chance after chance to turn back to him and repent. He's doing the same with us now. He wants us to seek him, love him, give our lives to him. But one day, a day

[40] Matthew 24:42-44.

known to God alone, that chance will run out, our earthly life will end.' And I think again how thankful I am, how overwhelmed with gratitude that Robbie was prepared, had already committed himself to God.

The counsellor takes up her glass of water. I glance at the clock. I am doing OK for time.

'After Robbie's accident, I read several books about people claiming they'd been to heaven. They gave me a brief comfort. But I was also a bit wary, conscious that I was desperate for descriptions of heaven and ready to believe anything.'

'That's understandable.'

'I came across a book by Eli Sheldon: *Near Death: A Biblical Journey*[41]. Do you know it?'

The counsellor looks at me intently. 'Possibly,' she says. 'Tell me a bit about it, then it might come to me.'

'Well, he talks about three main ideas regarding biblical accounts of death. He names them the "Concept of Continued Consciousness", the "Concept of Eternity" (or the "Thin Veil") and the "Concept of Being Received".' I count them on my fingers. 'Sheldon explains that verse in John where Jesus talks about us living, even though we die, if we believe in him.[42] He says that what Jesus means is that our spiritual being, our mental awareness, will never die. In his book he uses more than thirty years of research into near death experiences and hearing words spoken at the point of death. These are really worth reading,' I tell the counsellor. 'Sheldon believes that as the body passes from life to death, we maintain a constant conscious state. Our spiritual awareness is continuous from this life to the next. This is the first "Concept".'

I glance at the counsellor and go on. 'The "Concept of Continued Eternity" or the "Thin Veil" is based on the belief that eternity isn't somewhere for the future, for when we die, but that eternal life begins the moment we receive Jesus into our life and become a believer in him.'

I read out from my phone. 'This is John 5 verse 24: "Very truly I tell you, whoever hears my word and believes him who sent me has eternal life and will not be judged but has crossed over from death to life." Sheldon describes this as a thin veil separating our earthly life from the eternal one. The veil's in place from the day that we accept Jesus as Lord.

---

[41] *Near Death: A Biblical Journey;* Eli H. Sheldon.

[42] See John 11:25.

So for Robbie, that was when he was a teenager. Every day we walk one step closer to the veil until one day we just step through. Our life's a continuum. It doesn't stop at the point of bodily death but endures on into eternity.'

'That's interesting,' the counsellor voices.

'I like the way Sheldon puts this – in terms of securing a hotel booking or a place in heaven. The credit card (giving our life to Jesus) is given in advance to secure the booking, but the exact arrival time (death) is unknown. Whatever time that ends up being, the reservation is already in place and the price received (paid for by the blood of Jesus).'

'That's a useful analogy to remember.'

'Yes. And Sheldon's third "Concept" is "Being Received".'

The Bible App is ready. I scan the familiar words and read them out. '"Do not let your hearts be troubled. You believe in God; believe also in me. My Father's house has many rooms; if that were not so, would I have told you that I am going there to prepare a place for you? And if I go and prepare a place for you, I will come back and take you to be with me that you also may be where I am."[43] That's John 14,' I say. 'Sheldon points out in his book that the exact wording is often overlooked. It actually states that Jesus will *personally* come and take us to heaven. How amazing! At no one point will we be alone. And at no point was Robbie alone.' I look up, searching the counsellor's face. 'That's the reassurance I so desperately need to hear.'

'There are some really comforting words in those passages you have just read out.'

'Yes. The passage in John 11, verses 25 and 26, is on Robbie's stone in Mays Lane.'

And now my mind is back there again, to those harrowing days. So many impossible decisions to be made – like 1st July. It's not at all easy to talk about 1st July; to share with the counsellor about Robbie's service; to use that word 'funeral' that I find so upsetting.

'I try not to go back there in my head and that's one reason why we moved churches. But there was a real togetherness for our little family that day. We held each other's hands as we sat in the front room and prayed for strength to get through the day.' Images instantly crowd my mind. 'But snapshots, still frames, often creep into my head: the packed

---

[43] John 14:1-3.

church; the wonderful testimonies; the outpouring of music; Nigey stretching both his arms as wide as he could to reach us all, to encompass us all within his love.'

But what I hang on to, what I hold in my heart, isn't for sharing…

> I am in the pew, somehow still standing. Suddenly, spectacularly, wondrously, the sun is breaking through, its rays reaching down, illuminating only a specific ribbon of the church. It is that place containing my son. He is bathed in light, bathed in glory. He is safe.

'It's been vital for us all as a family to pull together and support each other – as we did before but also in a new way, mindful of lost family relationships that can't be replaced, memories we only shared with Robbie, where there is now no one to reminisce with.'

'Of course.'

'To see each other broken has been traumatic – as a mother, not to be able to protect my son and now not able to shield the others from heartache and pain.' My voice is being to wobble. I try to lift myself. 'We need help! We need to be supported by people who take on that role which Robbie had for us, being a son, being a big brother, being a friend.'

The counsellor is smiling.

I wrestle to explain what I mean. 'In the Bible there are plenty of examples of where others step in. Take Mary, for instance, Jesus' mother. It's hard to comprehend how much she must have suffered, how confused she must have been when the time came for Jesus to die. But God didn't forget her. When Jesus was on the cross and he saw his mother and "the disciple whom he loved", he told the disciple to look after her.[44] How incredible that in the midst of his great torment and physical pain, Jesus still remembered and cared for those he loved!

'In the Book of Ruth, Naomi lost her husband and both of her sons. She decided to return to her home in Judah, leaving her two daughters-in-law with their own families. But Ruth, one of them, refused to leave her. She showed unwavering love, kindness and support and returned to Judah with Naomi.[45] And in the story of David, when he was so upset at

---

[44] See John 19:25-27.
[45] Ruth 2:11.

the death of his great friend Jonathan, he looked around to see if there was anyone from Jonathan's household that he could support and love in Jonathan's place. That's how he made sure that Jonathan's son – long name I can't remember! – was provided for, restoring his lands and inviting him and all his household to eat with him every day.[46]

'I don't think there was time for you to read this last time,' I say, handing over a sheet of paper. 'This tribute to Robbie was written by two of his pupils, Sarah and Anoushka, in Year 10. What encouraging words – that they say they aspire to live their lives to the fullest in memory of Robbie and his inspirational achievements!'

The counsellor reads from the paper. '"Mr Schofield was an inspiration who enhanced the lives of everyone who was blessed enough to be a part of his life. He genuinely cared hugely for every single one of us and we looked upon him as not only a terrific teacher, but as a friend. His ability to please and make even the saddest person laugh will be cherished, and we are so very grateful for the impact he has had on us. He was such a beautiful and much-loved person who was always willing to give and expected nothing in return, which showed what an amazing person he really was. 'Mr Scho' was a role model whom everyone looked up to and without him the school is feeling strangely empty – a key piece is missing that can never be replaced. He has left so many fond memories and has imprinted his kindness on to our hearts. Mr Scho was a comic genius who brought out the best in everyone and was so easy to relate to. We will never forget his claims of not understanding teenagers whenever we did something bizarre that made him laugh, when actually, he understood us more than we understood ourselves. He always said he admired teenagers so much, but now he has the biggest admiration from us. His legacy will forever remain with us and we aspire to live our lives to the fullest in memory of him and his inspirational achievements. Each of us can remember a time when he personally told us to be more confident, stress less and not put so much pressure on ourselves to be perfect, which we will try our best to achieve as this is what he would have wanted. Mr Scho wanted the best for everyone. His trademark bow ties will always hold a place in our hearts – as he said, 'If you're gonna make a statement, make a statement!' whenever we criticised his unique dress sense! I don't think anyone will forget the transfer from his winter

---

[46] 2 Samuel 9.

uniform of a three-piece suit to his 'summer attire' in February consisting of a blue and white striped blazer and bow tie, with the excuse, 'This is what happens when I go shopping on my own.' Mr Scho started the iPad cult at Farnborough Hill amongst the teachers, even though he himself refused to fix his cracked screen, forever coming up with a different excuse why. Mr Scho will be greatly missed at Farnborough Hill yet his unique impact of good will, will forever remain. His love for educating, and not just academically, will be a part of us as we grow up. And, to quote this truly loved man, 'You're all stars – literally.'"'

> There is a hurricane in Florida, the knock-on effect meaning the seas around the Menai Straits are pretty wild and not the ideal conditions for Robbie to be working on getting his Sailing Instructor's Certificate.
>
> I have a chat with God about keeping Robbie safe in the rough seas and add a plea that Robbie will be able to finish the course – and also to pass. The time when he wasn't able to complete his Spinnaker Level, one school holiday at Burghfield, due to lack of wind, is forever etched in my mind; he was most definitely not happy.
>
> Digbeth coach station in Birmingham has certainly improved from when I was a teenager, but it's not a place I would like to hang around in, I think as I lean against the iron railings waiting for Robbie's coach to pull in. We will be going straight to my parents for a family summer gathering and I am still praying for good news as, at last, the coach pulls in. I can see Robbie's head bent face down as he negotiates the steps. Now he looks up – a huge beam at me as he gathers up his bag from the pavement where the driver is busy emptying the contents of the boot – and strides over.
>
> 'Nailed it! Got my Power Boat Certificate and I'm a qualified Sailing Instructor.'
>
> I reach to give him a hug and send up a silent *thank you.*

'You see, I believe that not only are others called to step in when we lose someone, but that we're also called to continue the work that they were doing. So for Robbie, that may mean sailing, teaching, working with the youth, worshipping God through music, being generous with our time, reaching out to others, making others laugh, supporting them. And many other things.'

The counsellor nods. 'That's a lovely idea.'

'It's like that Basílica in Barcelona, that large Roman Catholic church designed by Gaudi. When he died, less than a quarter of the building was complete. But then others have taken on the challenge of continuing the work. Despite not being finished still, the place's now a UNESCO world heritage site. That's amazing!'

I think of places in the Bible where others were called to take over; Joshua appointed to continue the journey to the Promised Land after Moses was taken to be with God, the disciples called to continue the ministry of Jesus after his death. Although, I also note that Moses did eventually reach the Promised Land hundreds of earthly years later.[47] Is this a case of someone finishing their work *after* their death, I wonder?

Later, on my way home, the counselling session replaying in my head, I'm suddenly reminded of a poem that I love. It conjures up some of the things I was trying to explain to the counsellor. Robbie is physically unavailable to me but *he is alive.* He's crossed the thin veil and is no longer visible to me, but he's just a breath away. I wish I'd shared the poem with her.

Perspective[48]

I am standing alone on the seashore.
A ship spreads his sails to the morning breeze,
and starts for the ocean.
I stand watching him until he fades on the horizon.
And someone at my side says, 'He is gone!'
Gone where? The loss of sight is in me, not in him.
At that moment when someone says, 'He is gone!'
There are others who are watching him coming.
Other voices take up the glad shout,
'Here he comes!'
And that is dying.

---

[47] This occurred during the Transfiguration in Luke 9:28-36.

[48] *Perspective;* Sir Henry Scott Holland.
The poem has been abridged and 'she' has been changed to 'he' to make it more personal.

I'm in the kitchen clearing up when I hear the sound of keys in the door.

Someone is charging down the stairs calling, 'Look who's here!'

My heart is thumping. I'm holding my breath.

'Who is it?' I call. Hoping. Longing. Yearning.

'Just us.'

My face falls, my arms drop, my heart sinks. Not Robbie then. Not Robbie again.

SESSION 13

Resilience

'It sounds like so much has happened in the space of the last few years and is happening still – lots of difficult situations that you have had to manage, that you are still having to manage.'

'Although you feel like you can't go on, that the world has stopped, of course life *does* still keep happening, whether you want it to or not. Exactly one week after the accident was Jack's birthday, and he got his degree results while the vicar was round planning his brother's funeral. Attending Jack's graduation just four weeks later was another incredibly hard thing. But I managed somehow to contain my anxiety and not have a panic attack in the Great Hall. And not long after was Millie's eighteenth.'

The counsellor gives me a sympathetic look, nods and waits for me to continue.

'And that's what happens. You somehow manage to seem OK on the outside when inside you are falling apart. I've become an expert at appearing to be one thing, seeming as though I am coping, when the reality is completely the opposite. I can mostly put on this public front when I am out, deal with situations, work, social things, hearing other people's good news, family gatherings, special occasions. But it's when I get back home, when the door shuts, that I break down.'

> Nigey's niece is getting married. Today. But I am not there. I am at home. Alone. It is nearing the end of August and my emotions are far too raw to attend a wedding a handful of weeks after I should have been at another that now won't happen; *will never happen.* I am delighted for Nigey's niece and her husband-to-be. But I can't be there, can't join the others. Instead I am knitting. Knitting and knitting and knitting. A slow rhythmic,

repetitive action that is comforting and familiar; that absorbs enough of my concentration to force out other things, but is not too demanding so that I am overwhelmed. I want to be alone. I am worn out with all the talking; going over and over and over everything again and again with the same people, with different people, with family, with myself. I crave nothingness, emptiness, no demands, no expectations. I don't answer the phone when it starts ringing. I don't go to the door. I want to shut everything out.

'It sounds like you reached a point when you needed your own space – to push away the things that had been all-consuming.'

'In the immediate aftermath, we were swamped with visitors. That time is all such a blur. Each day there were a different number of people for dinner. Endless cups of tea. We took to using paper plates when the dishwasher packed in. And so many flowers and cards and promises of help. And then one day I couldn't do it anymore. There's nothing to say about that. I just simply couldn't do it. I stopped replying to texts and left the door unopened. We still often don't answer the phone. I know it was hard for some of our friends to understand, and I didn't have the words to explain to them.'

'And how are things with your friends now?'

'Well, the strange thing is that although some friends did stick with us, and I'm so grateful to them for that, others we hardly see now. Socialising became a huge issue for me. I lost so much confidence. I became fearful of what a conversation would hold: that I might have to listen to stories of accidents, or deal with questions about my family, or hear how wonderfully life was treating other people. But I have got stronger. And we've made new friends and have a new support network.'

I watch as the rain batters against the window and streams of water race down the pane. How can I explain to the counsellor how much I need support from others yet long to be alone?

It is all too much, too difficult, too hard to manage. Too many complicated feelings. I have absolutely nothing left to give. My body is empty, my emotions mixed into a tangle I don't have the energy to unpick. I have only one thing that is driving me on: I have to get out. I have to run away. I can't deal with everything anymore. I can hear Nigey calling for me, asking me where I am going; but I don't stop, I don't answer. The next thing, I am in the car. Driving. I have no idea where to. It is dark and I am suddenly so tired, overcome with weariness. The tears are almost blinding. And I am worn out. Exhausted. And cold now too as I sit huddled in my coat in the dim lights of the village car park. I crave sleep; to shut out this world that has become unbearable. But I don't sleep. I don't drive on. I start the engine and make my way back home. Some force is urging me on. Running away is not the answer.

'I know it was and is so difficult for others to know how to be there for me when I didn't know what I wanted myself. I had no idea what help would help, and what help would just become another burden. And people often assumed that because I still had Nigey, still had Jack and Tabby and Millie, that would be OK.'

The counsellor nods.

'And although we were so strong together in those early days, I found it very hard that we all coped with our grief in different ways. It looked like some of the family were moving on too quickly, managing fine without Robbie, leaving him behind. But of course, I did want them to get on with their own lives too. Then at other times, their grief would gush out, as though they had let it build up rather than releasing it as a steady flow.'

'Yes, there are so many ways to deal with grief and, as you say, we are all different and manage in different ways.'

'And, of course, we all had our own relationship with Robbie. He'd been a part of all our lives in different ways and we also had the extra complication of being a blended family.'

I pause for a moment, thinking back.

'Losing a child puts a massive strain on a marriage. Nigey and I had already been through so much in the past few years. And because we had lost his parents, we didn't have that area of support; and because my sister had been through so much with her brain haemorrhage and losing her husband, my own parents needed to support her as much as they could. There have been so many pressures on us. But, thanks to God, our marriage is another thing which has been refined and strengthened through our loss.'

'Yes, I can see how losing Robbie has impacted on so many areas of your life.'

'It's difficult to explain, but after a while you kind of feel this invisible pressure to get back to living again; after a certain timeframe the accident wasn't talked about. It's as though we were expected to have "moved on". It's something I feel pretty strongly about – that this country can't do grief.'

I'm angry, disappointed, let down by the lack of awareness.

'I came across this article[49] the other day about how some countries cope with death by having long periods of mourning or certain rituals. The article questions the burden we put on people here – that it's expected they should rush back to work after the funeral. Despite the emotional cost, we feel pressurised to soldier on and be back to "normal" within weeks. In other countries the bereaved are supported, comforted…' I struggle to find the right word, to voice this pent-up frustration. '*Recognised.* That's it. We need grief to be recognised, not brushed away as soon as is decently possible. After all, it's a fact of life. The one certainty after we're born is that we'll die; it affects us all.'

I sit forwards. My head is pounding. I feel so passionately about all this.

> I am at the surgery – again. It seems like my second home.
>
> I am torn, divided about how I find this fact. On one hand, I am so grateful to the kind doctor who has been there for me – listening, patient, sympathetic. I feel so nurtured, so tended for, that she has recognised my great distress; that she has wanted to see me fortnightly; that she has cared. But I also feel angry, trampled on, packaged up and labelled. My head knows she thinks she is helping.
>
> I have been feeling low, tearful, helpless; I have lost interest in life – and for more than six months since that horrendous day. So I have antidepressants. It's what is expected. It's how the doctor has been trained. My heart knows that I will always ache, always struggle, always have that gaping hole that will never be filled.

---

[49] *Have the British Forgotten How to Grieve;* Clover Stroud. *www.telegraph.co.uk/news/health/10639359/Have-the-British-forgotten-how-to-grieve.html*

And taking pills isn't the answer. My reaction is *normal.* I have lost my son. Of course I don't feel on top of the world.

The buzzer is sounding. My name is on the screen – my turn to go in. It's time for my usual fight with the doctor. I have stopped taking the tablets and she isn't pleased. I go to work; I look after myself, look after the family; I interact in the world. But she still wants me to take the pills. It is a battle that I am winning because, thankfully, I am in control. But it shouldn't be like this. I shouldn't be made to feel that I'm abnormal; that the fact life is still so hard is somehow wrong; that by taking medication I can make everything right again.

'So,' the counsellor addresses me gently, summing up in a few words, 'you feel upset that this country doesn't understand grief?'

'Yes. I realise that antidepressants are needed sometimes and that's fine of course. But it just all seems too easy to hand over a few drugs and expect that'll solve everything. I found a recent research paper about bereavement. They interviewed people who'd lost someone through suicide or another form of traumatic death (except loss through a train crash or terrorism, as then there's usually national mourning). They felt that they could only show their grief for a limited time, after which they felt compelled to suppress their feelings. They felt that they weren't permitted the space and acceptance to grieve as they needed to.'

'So that's something you feel too?'

'Oh, yes. I can certainly relate to that. In the research paper, they refer to several real-life cases. One of these is the story of Mark – I *think* that was his name – who lost his life when the car he was overtaking on his motorbike turned right. The testimony from his mother shows how she struggled with being allowed to express her grief. She's quoted as saying how unbelievable she found it that people thought the funeral would bring closure. The study's conclusion is that a vital factor in trying to make sense of traumatic loss is being given the permission and space to grieve.'

I pause and put my hand up instinctively to the necklace I wear of Robbie's thumbprint.

'I've stopped telling people Robbie was on a motorbike,' I inform the counsellor. 'There's a different reaction to saying a "road accident" rather than a "motorbike accident". With the motorbike, there's that knowing look and a shaking of the head and the assumption that the fact he was on a motorbike is to some degree to blame. But it wasn't his fault. The point that he was on a motorbike should be irrelevant.' But what I don't say again is that I know in my heart of hearts that if he'd been in his Land Rover that day, the outcome would've been very different; he was so vulnerable on his motorbike. Still, there is a stigmatism.

The whole of the table is covered in paper – in piles, in single sheets, stapled together, folded, highlighted; strewn around. The doors to the garden are open, a very gentle breeze hardly disturbing the disarray. My younger sister is here. I am so thankful to her that she is sorting the next wad of paperwork.

The call to the mobile company, cancelling Robbie's phone, has just about finished me. I had buoyed myself up, planned the words in my head, forced myself to make the call – another company, another person, another organisation needing to be told. But the man hadn't listened to me. He'd told me he couldn't discuss details of someone else's account without their permission. Despite me having repeated in great distress several times that Robbie couldn't give permission because he had died, the man asked if I could put Robbie on the phone so he could talk to him. I had to leave Nigey to finish the call, unable to contain my anguish, my tears, my rage.

'Here you go, Netta,' Nigey is saying to my sister now, handing her the form. 'This is the teaching union that Robbie paid in to every month. This is the policy doc. You see it states that it pays compensation if a teacher loses their life travelling to or from school. So Robbie must be covered as he was going to school.'

She nods and takes the things from him.

But it isn't good news. She puts the phone down on the table and comes out to the garden to join us. 'It's unbelievable – but there's a clause in the small print that stipulates that no compensation will be awarded if the teacher was on a motorbike.'

'So that means if, like Robbie, you're exercising your free will to ride a bike, keeping to the law, and the accident is proved in court not to be your fault, you get nothing.' As I talk to the counsellor, I realise that this is yet another area where I still feel angry. 'There are all these feelings still bubbling away inside me,' I say, 'and I am acutely aware that grief can be so all-consuming that it can cloud your vision, channel your thoughts inwards, centre everything on yourself and your situation; make you self-focused, self-absorbed, to the exclusion of everything else. There's a danger that it can make you bitter and resentful.'

The counsellor pulls her cardigan together over her chest and folds her arms. 'Are you thinking that might be a danger for you?'

'Well…' I start. This isn't easy to answer. 'I hope not. I'm aware of the danger but also know that losing Robbie has without question changed me. I don't want to be bitter. I don't want to be defined by my loss but rather by having Robbie still living in my heart, be full of love as he was.'

I change tack, taking the spotlight off myself. 'Keller, the one who wrote *Walking with God Through Pain and Suffering,* refers to Daniel's friends in the furnace and says that, when we suffer, when we're in our own fiery furnace, we have two choices: either to let the flames harden and break us or let the fire reshape and refine.'

'From the Book of Daniel?'

'Yes, in the Old Testament, the story of King Nebuchadnezzar. There's a mouthful! The King had a huge golden statue erected and commanded the people to worship it. Three Jewish men, Daniels's friends, refused, so the King ordered them to be thrown into a blazing furnace.'

'Ah, yes,' the counsellor says.

'When the friends told the King that God would rescue them, he became very angry and had the fire made seven times hotter than before, so that the heat even killed the soldiers who threw the men in. But the amazing thing was that the men weren't harmed at all. And there was a fourth man seen in the furnace walking round with the others.[50] It's a story that illustrates Jesus' presence, even in our suffering. He's in it with us.'

'Yes, that's amazing, like you say.'

'Keller also picks up that the passage in Daniel shows not only that Jesus is with us, but that he doesn't just sit with us in it; he walks with us, moves with us. In other words, Jesus helps us to keep going, helps us

---

[50] See Daniel 3:24-25.

to wade through. We don't have to stay stuck wallowing in our pain. Although it will still stay with us, we can move through it.

'There are lots of other examples in the Bible which capture this idea of Jesus keeping us active. I've bookmarked loads of passages: Psalm 23:4 – "Even though I walk through the darkest valley, I will fear no evil, for you are with me." Isaiah 50:10 – "Let the one who walks in the dark, who has no light, trust in the name of the Lord." And another from Isaiah... Isaiah 43:2 – "When you walk through the fire, you will not be burned."'

After reading these to the counsellor, I look up and put my mobile down. 'Thing is, it all sounds great but, practically, how do you do it? In his book Keller talks about everyday experiences and emotions and finding God through these – things like crying, trusting, praying, loving, hoping. And I've thought about a few more to add to his list: forgiving, finding peace, finding joy. And worshipping.'

> We are down by the river. It's past 10pm and very dark. There is no one around but us. Christmas Eve by the River Thames.
>
> I have got through the day, detached and disconnected, empty inside from my outbursts the night before full of fearful anticipation. I have managed to get through Robbie's birthday. *We* have managed to get through Robbie's birthday. He should be twenty-seven today. We have done all the usual things from past years, like going out to lunch, and had family and friends round. Except it is startlingly different. There are no presents to begin the day, no joyous texts. Instead, we have been to Mays Lane and left cards there. Lit the candles. Robbie isn't here. And now, exhausted, drained, I am standing on the wide-open sweep of grassland by the river with the others.
>
> Nigey is wrestling with the Chinese lantern; Tabby is grappling with the match; Jack has his pen at hand, ready. And I watch as the lantern is borne aloft, pulled upwards by a tug of wind, out across the vast emptiness of the night sky, higher and higher, farther and farther. Until now only a speck of light remains. The words to Robbie, the messages written on the lantern, are carried away. Free.

'It's stating the obvious,' I am telling the counsellor, 'that Christmas and Robbie's birthday are incredibly hard days to get through. And the build-up before, the dread of what's to come, can be even worse.'

'There is no right or wrong thing to do. You just have to try to manage in whatever way you can,' the counsellor says.

'Last year, in early December, Nigey and I went away to Suffolk. We stayed in a cottage in a tiny village about a mile across the fields to the sea. The first morning, we woke early, got dressed and walked along the deserted path, a huge expanse of empty landscape spread out before us. En route to the sea, the sun rose, flooding the sky with brilliant light, illuminating the golden reeds lining our path. It was stunning. Next day, we got up even earlier so that we could be on the beach to watch the sun rising. It's those moments, those wonderful glimpses of the sheer beauty and wonder of the natural world, that can give a glimmer of joy, even in the midst of utter hopelessness.'

'A lovely moment.' The counsellor is smiling at me.

'Yes. It was punishingly cold; the wind was vicious. But it was definitely worth it! And another time in Suffolk we went out into the night, down the path towards the sea to watch the stars. It was breathtaking; "totally awesome", to use one of Robbie's phrases; a visual reminder of who we are in all of creation, of our place in the universe. It was a reminder of how insignificant we are, yet how much we mean to God, what he's done for us – and that somewhere out there is Robbie.'

The counsellor nods.

'I know that it's the small things – a thoughtful word, a new flower out in the garden, a hug, a comforting text – that make all the difference. But I've never fully appreciated that, never taken it on board as much as I do now. The joy of a new rose or my seedlings germinating can carry me through the day.' I think of 'Robbie's garden', as I like to call it, in the cemetery at Mays Lane. 'There's something uplifting about being in the open air, about being among nature.'

The counsellor nods again.

'In the early days, certainly, it was so helpful to have a place to go – to be able to go to Mays Lane – to have a focus; to be tending his garden, nurturing it, watering it, creating something, caring. That's about the only thing I can do for him now. And it means I can incorporate something physical for Robbie within my week.'

But as I call in there en route for home, it's never an easy place to visit. I think about how Jesus, on the eve of his arrest and crucifixion, spoke to his disciples about how to keep going. It's in John 15:4. Jesus repeatedly uses the word 'remain'. And I think that's what I need to do: stick with him whatever, just as he sticks with me.

I'm walking to work when I hear it approach.

Someone is driving down the street.

My heart is thumping. I'm holding my breath.

Right model. Right colour. Snorkel exhaust. I watch. Hoping. Longing. Yearning.

Just a Land Rover. Just another Land Rover.

My face falls, my arms drop, my heart sinks. Not Robbie then. Not Robbie again.

Session 14

Resolution

'I cried all the way through the court hearings, in the Magistrates Court and the Crown Court. Especially during the sentencing. I was determined to stay in there but it was incredibly hard to control myself, to not break down completely.'

The counsellor offers me another tissue.

> I have beaten myself up about whether or not I should go to court, whether or not I should see the car driver. Kelly and Dick have taken us through everything and explained what will happen. They have put no pressure on me at all; the decision is entirely mine. But how totally impossible to know what to do. In the end, I think I would rather regret going, than not go and then later wish I had.
>
> It is a surreal day. I sit at work in the morning, finding it easier to focus here than panic by myself at home.
>
> We arrive at court with Kelly and Dick, very early so that there is time for us to be shown inside the courtroom and taken through what will happen. We are told that every case starts at the Magistrates Court. It is an intimate space, with just a row of chairs along the wall for family and friends. We wait back outside until 2pm. I want my body to react, to respond to the emotion that is choking me inside. But instead, unbelievably, I am chatting to Kelly and Dick about cooking and family holidays.

'Yes, that must have been a very difficult decision to make.'

'I thought the face of the car driver would be etched forever in my mind. I held the door open for this young chap to go into court and I knew instantly it must be him. How are you supposed to feel, to react to someone whose car killed your son?' I pause, trying to think how to go on, to explain that you feel everything and yet nothing at all. 'And his parents sat a couple of seats along from us next to Dick and Kelly. My eyes were fixed on him the whole time and of course I saw him at the two subsequent court appearances, but his face amazingly has dimmed and blurred. I don't know if I would recognise him now if we passed in the street... To hear the magistrate summing up what had happened, I cried and cried. You'd have thought by the time of the sentencing in January, at the Crown Court after his guilty plea, that I'd have used up all my tears, but I cried and cried then too.'

> It is a rollercoaster of emotions. I am full of apprehension on arrival but that is quickly replaced by anger when, before court, I hear that the car driver's defence will be that he was looking down at his speedometer.
>
> And now I am anxious again, sitting on a hard, wooden pew in court with my family – waiting, waiting, waiting; forty-five minutes of waiting, a delay before the sentencing can commence.
>
> Now the prosecution is outlining their case. I am tense, rigid, stiff with pent-up emotion; holding my breath... And then suddenly a sharp plummeting, a sinking, a feeling of deep despair; the judge doesn't agree that the case is in the 'middle band' of careless driving. I feel sick, exhausted, panicked. I am waiting to hear that the judge believes it should be in a lower category. In those few seconds, I am utterly desolated; wrung out. But the judge isn't taking things in that direction. He thinks the case falls just short of dangerous driving.
>
> The parts of our Victim Impact Statement that have been permitted are being read to the court. Neither Kelly nor Dick have ever come across a case where the Defence have objected to parts of the statement. And now the tears are flowing. It is so real to hear it all being read out. I am on the verge of hysteria, struggling to hold in the screams, to keep some kind of composure so I don't have to leave court. But the tears won't be contained. They are running down my face, pouring out everything I have left.

'He heals the broken-hearted and binds up their wounds,' I read out from my phone. 'That's from Psalm 147. It makes me feel warm inside – wrapped up and loved.'

'Yes, it's beautifully worded.'

'Kandiah, remember him?' I laugh. 'He's the one who wrote *Paradoxology*. Well, he looks at Job and suggests we all should do the same when we're hurting and bewildered with God; that is, to take our pain and questions to him.'

For some reason it makes me think about when Robbie was little; about how independent and self-sufficient he was, but how good it made me feel when he did need me, when he had fallen over and bumped himself or when he wasn't well. Those were the times when he turned to me and I was the one who could give comfort. And I think how much God longs to do the same with us when we're hurting.

'Keller, now he has a lot to say about this lamenting to God.'

'Remind me who Keller is…'

'He wrote *Walking with God Through Pain and Suffering*. He says that many of the psalms in the Bible are about pouring out anxieties and troubles without holding back. There are two psalms in particular he writes about. Psalms 39 and 88 are full of deep distress, with no words of comfort or hope even by the end. There's three things Keller notes. First, that there's no quick fix and even when we plead with God, suffering can persist. Second, God understands our desperation and despair. He didn't delete psalms like this but felt they had a place as part of his word. And third, by continuing to call on God even though nothing seems to be changing, it's a demonstration of loving God for who he is rather than what he can give us.'

The counsellor nods and waits for me to continue.

'With life being thrown upside down, I've had to learn to trust God, to put myself in his hands. Since losing Robbie, I changed my role at work, Nigey's job went through restructuring with the threat of redundancy and I was faced with the same thing.'

I note the empathy in the counsellor's face as she sits forward to hear more.

'Nigey had to apply for a new role. It was all incredibly stressful, especially the "not knowing". He was concerned that his current job would cease to exist under the new structure, and in the end, he was right. I tried to tell myself it would be fine and we could move somewhere new, somewhere cheaper if necessary. But the thought of leaving the home where Robbie grew up left me panicked and afraid.'

'And what was *your* role change at work?'

'Well, I was working visiting families as part of my research role in child anxiety. I just felt I couldn't face that anymore. I couldn't guarantee I wouldn't start crying at something they said, and didn't want to hear or have to deal with all their problems. I was too worried about driving to travel the long distances that job required. Initially, I dropped my hours and took on a more co-ordinating office-based role but I still spoke to families on the phone. When the funding ended, I couldn't cope with the thought of doing research again, but couldn't face the thought seven months after the accident of having to move to a new place of work, somewhere unfamiliar. So, when an admin job came up at work, I applied. It was a drop of two grades, a huge pay cut, and full time. The longer hours were such a struggle and I wasn't coping well. Then all of those supporting roles at work were restructured and I wasn't sure I would even have a job. There was so much uncertainty and worry. But thankfully I do, and I was able to take that chance to cut my hours to four days.'

I think how those few words spoken to the counsellor don't even begin to convey all the extra pressure and burden that the work situation heaped on us.

'It's been an area where I've been hugely challenged. I hadn't realised how hard I'd find it climbing down the ladder – how much it would hurt to see my pay cut in half, on top of all the other costs, emotional and financial, of losing someone.'

'You've had so much to deal with,' the counsellor is telling me.

But I already know this, already know that I have only managed to stay standing because God's hand has been holding me up. It's by trusting in God that I'm learning all sorts of things about myself and about him too; about my priorities and about what's important; about who I am.

'It's a challenge to keep trusting when so many things don't turn out like you think they will.'

Robbie is upstairs on the computer, phone in hand, trying to get through. It's early still but already the day has contained enough emotion to last the week. A level results. Disappointment. Rejection. Reappraisal. Acceptance. Achievement. Success. Joy. It has been a see-saw ride. His first choice of Bath won't consider him. He has just missed the required grades. It's a top university for mechanical and automotive engineering, places are competitive, and unless you meet their grade specification to be in, you're out. There is no negotiating. It's difficult to discern how Robbie is feeling. Running parallel to this story of despondency is one of hope: Birmingham want him. They are his second choice but have offered him a place unconditionally. It is a wonderful tribute to Robbie's steely determination and grit that when he had to dig deep, when life was tough in the sixth form, he rose to the challenge. And now he has been rewarded, just not in the way that he planned.

'When Robbie didn't get into Bath Uni, he was disappointed, of course. I went round the Open Day there with him. It was where he really wanted to go. But looking back, with all the medical problems that Robbie faced at university, with the major bowel surgery, it was good he was in Birmingham and not in Bath. His grandparents are there. When Robbie went back to uni after his hospital stay and recovery at home, the lecturers thought it best that he forfeited the rest of his second year and repeated the year. He decided against this. So having the support of my parents then and at other times was just so wonderful.' It was a case, I think, of trusting that God knows best, of God knowing the bigger picture.

The counsellor smiles. 'Yes, that worked out well in the end.'

'It's like the Old Testament story of Joseph, in Genesis. So many tragedies happen over many years. But in the end, Joseph's faith in God is rewarded and he becomes the means through which many people are saved. It's a great story to illustrate how seemingly no-hope situations can be turned around by God. It's also a good reminder to me personally about being patient in the bad times, about waiting on God, trusting in him and letting him into each and every situation.'

But there is another bad time.

I lean forwards in my chair, glance at the counsellor and then beyond her, to the window and the tops of the trees. It is a peaceful, calm scene – so far removed from another awful day, another difficult memory.

> I am completely, utterly, totally out of control. Beyond myself. I am hysterical, berserk. I am beyond reach. Frenzied. And I am screaming, shrieking, screeching; yelling at the top of my voice. It is less than a year since I lost Robbie and I am going to lose them both. I am about to lose Jack too. Both my precious sons, taken. There is nothing Nigey can say, nothing *anyone* can say. I am inconsolable. I am delirious. I am entirely consumed, eaten up with fear. I am finished.

'So, this incident that happened. You thought you had lost Jack too?'

I nod. I can't talk any more about it. The reality of what might have been is too horrendous to revisit.

> I am praying, shouting at God, furious with him, pleading with him, begging. Desperate. Distraught. And he *does* listen. He *does* respond. He *does* answer. Jack is OK.

'Pete Greig's *God on Mute*[51] is a really useful book about prayer. I only came across it recently. I can't remember how; maybe someone mentioned it in church. Anyway, he writes a lot about unanswered prayer and perseverance. It's a book I would recommend to anyone: full of information, examples, personal testimony, and easy to read too; an incredibly honest look at why God can often seem silent and unresponsive to our prayers.'

There is silence in the room. Then the counsellor comments, 'Yes, I think I know that book.'

'And then, of course, there are those prayers that *are* answered, just not in the way that we've envisaged. Like with Robbie going to Birmingham and not Bath Uni. And God keeping him safe on his journey to school, that I've talked about before. I love the image that this Bible verse conjures up,' I say, reading out from my phone. 'Matthew 11:28: "Come to me, all you who are weary and burdened, and I will give you rest." And James 5:13 tells us, "Is anyone among you in trouble? Let them pray." It's what it's all about – taking everything to God in prayer.'

I'm reminded about the prayer course we've been doing in home group – also a Pete Greig thing.

---

[51] *God on Mute;* Pete Greig.

'In Mark's Gospel, the blind man, Bartimaeus, cries out to Jesus.[52] Jesus asks him what he wants him to do. Jesus must know that Bartimaeus is blind. He must know that he craves healing and having his sight restored. But it's an example of how although God already knows our needs, we still need to ask – to pray to him.'

I look around the room. I've lost my train of thought. But the counsellor regards me kindly and waits for me to continue. This is happening a lot; my concentration is poor. I tear at the tissue in my lap, shred the soft white paper, and I wonder what to say, how to go on, how to explain, how to tell her about everything...

I think about my life now. How can I convey how contradictory it's become? I am desperate to run away but home is the only place I want to be. I want to merely exist, be in my own protective bubble, yet I want to live life to the full, taking nothing for granted, knowing how precious life is.

And how can I describe what I feel about sleep, that it is longed for yet dreaded; the yearning to block everything out but the long difficult hours in the middle of the night before oblivion comes; the need to shut out all those intrusive images that frighten and consume me? In my mind, the accident is played out in slow motion, scene by scene, so vivid, so real, when I wasn't even there. And especially at night, when the pain in my chest is at its most intense, when there is no place to find comfort physically or emotionally. I have become a champion of knowledge, lying awake trying to force my mind onto other things. I can now recite all the states of America, all the trees beginning with each letter of the alphabet, different types of biscuits, the words of poems, songs, Bible verses... *anything* to channel my mind away from that horror. But it is exhausting.

I look up and tell the counsellor, 'God has been my strength, been there in the quiet of the night when my heart is aching and my tortured mind won't still.'

I cross my legs and twist a strand of hair around my fingers.

'It's easy to think of peace as an overwhelming calmness, an absence of trouble; that it's tranquillity.'

The counsellor nods.

---

[52] See Mark 10:51.

'But Paul explains to the Philippians that as well as this, God's peace is also a feeling of being looked after and protected. Not an absence of painful thoughts, but a presence.[53]'

'Interesting,' the counsellor says. 'So how does that work?'

'Well, I think it means that it won't help to try and block out bad memories without dealing with them. We need to face them with God's help.'

The counsellor nods.

'Paul suggests three ways. So, number one, to think about, pray and read God's word; and consider that "bigger picture" we've talked about before that only God knows. Number two, be thankful, trying to thank God before we ask him for things, not just after we've got them! Keller adds that when we ask God for something, he'll always give us what we would've asked for if we knew the bigger picture. And Keller says that if we can believe this, it'll bring peace. And number three, Paul calls us to love: to love God, to love ourselves and to love other people. That means our partners, children, family, friends; even our enemies; but God is to be top of the list!'

The counsellor is watching me as I look up.

'I've found that a challenge in the past. It's so easy to make our loved ones all important. But it's something I'm learning to do: to love God supremely, above and beyond anything else, to put him first.' And, I think, I hope, by doing this, it may bring peace. 'But it's not easy,' I add, 'to find that peace. I've become really fearful of so many things.'

'Fearful? Of what sort of things?' the counsellor asks.

What, I think, apart from the obvious: the unspoken terror that as this has happened once, why not again?

> I am walking back from work. The day has been unremarkable. But I have made it through. I have started writing down every hour on a sticky note on my desk and crossing each one off when they have passed; breaking the day at work down into smaller, more manageable chunks. But I am anxious, frightened. The thought of tragedy striking again is tormenting me as I leave the campus and cross the road.

---

[53] Philippians 4:6-8,12.

> As I walk, suddenly I am overcome with a sense of Jesus; of a face close to mine before me, looking into my eyes. I sense that Jesus is with me, that he knows and understands this anguish, and that it won't happen again.

But these are not things I talk to the counsellor about. Despite the reassurance, it's something I don't ever want to give voice to.

The counsellor is waiting for me to explain.

'Images,' I begin, 'so many images that scare me. I had a panic attack before Tabby's graduation. I totally broke down in the hotel the night before, thinking about all the bones and skeletons that would be on show at the chiropractor's clinic, reminders of the reality I can't face. But anyone who saw me next day, smiling and delighted, would've had no idea of what terror the night before had held.'

I think of all the TV adverts and previews I struggle with too – how you can be watching a harmless quiz show and next moment some horrific scene of a car crash is happening right in front of you, billed as 'entertainment'. And the cinema is pretty much a no-go.

'I worry about holidays, about going far away from the children,' I tell the counsellor. 'Nigey and I have only been away nearby. I know that even if we hadn't been in Cyprus, even if I had just been in Reading that awful morning, I still would've been too late, still wouldn't have made it. But the holiday thing is a really difficult issue for me.'

The counsellor nods and I carry on.

'The ridiculous thing is that I can cope if the children go away, go abroad. But I have this block about going myself. My sister's told me that it's because if the children go away that's their decision, but if I go away then I am choosing to leave them. Whatever, it's another area where I need help.'

'I can see it's a struggle for you.'

'As a church we studied *Looking Through the Cross*[54] by Graham Tomlin as a Lent text. He writes that Jesus' self-sacrifice on the cross is the way of love. In Ezekiel, it says that through the resurrection, we'll be given a new heart and a new spirit – a heart of flesh, not a heart of stone.[55] Sounds wonderful! But a soft heart means more pain. There's a cost. The

[54] *Looking through the Cross;* Graham Tomlin.
[55] Ezekiel 36:26.

more you're able to love, the more you have to lose and the more vulnerable you are. A heart of stone is broken a lot less easily. A heart of stone would guard against suffering. But who'd want a life without love?'

'So, you're saying that to love is to risk getting hurt.'

I nod. 'But we can turn that full circle. If we have a heart of love, we may suffer, but we can also let our love reach out to others who may be facing similar things. You see, there's this story that Kushner mentions in his book. A woman who's lost her only son seeks help from a holy man. He simply tells her that in order to ease the sorrow in her own life, she needs to bring to him a mustard seed from a home that's never known heartbreak. The first home she tries has a long list of woes about all their troubles, and certainly isn't the home free from heartbreak that she's looking for. But she stays and supports them for a while as she feels an empathy after what she's been through. And of course, what happens is that every house she comes to, it turns out, has met with some kind of grief or sorrow. Instead of returning to the holy man with a mustard seed, the woman's thoughts are diverted from her own pain and redirected to helping those she meets.'

'Oh, what a lovely tale!'

'Yes! Certainly something to aspire to,' I answer.

All this is food for thought as I negotiate my way home.

I'm in the kitchen clearing up when the phone rings.

Someone is charging down the stairs calling, 'I'll get it!'

My heart is thumping. I'm holding my breath.

'Who is it?' I call. Hoping. Longing. Yearning.

'Just Sainsbury's. Running late.'

My face falls, my arms drop, my heart sinks. Not Robbie then. Not Robbie again.

SESSION 15

Restoration

I tell the counsellor how we have moved churches. 'Even now, church can be one of the hardest places for me to be,' I say. 'For me, the physical fabric of the building at our old church where we worshipped is caught up with Robbie's service on 1st July. So, we moved to worship elsewhere, somewhere that doesn't look so "churchy".'

'So that's another loss – the loss of your old church and all that went with it.'

I nod. 'Where we are now, the teaching is excellent and the worship can raise the roof. And I really needed to feel free to truly worship. But the pastoral care, the support, the space to talk about Robbie has, at times, been sadly missing. People only know the new Lizzie there, the different me, the person that I am now. And they didn't know Robbie.'

'Yes, that must be hard.'

'I hardly ever miss a Sunday and have only had to leave early a few times. But I frequently cry still – often feel the tears streaming. At home, sometimes, I manage by thinking that Robbie is just busy with his own life, as he used to be, as the others are, and I will see him soon. But every single week when I am in church and I sing about death, the stark reality hits me that he has gone, that there won't be his keys in the door again. As the lyrics speak of the grave, I can't avoid thinking of that place that I try so hard not to think about; as I watch the worship band, that his guitars will just keep on gathering dust and he won't play them again; as I hear others talk about miracles, that there was none for us; as I listen to the banns of marriage, watch the children being dedicated and christened, that this is no longer going to be part of the future I'd imagined for Robbie. It can be such a challenge to lift up my voice in joy, to sing about all God's blessings and greet my neighbour with a smile. But I'm trying so hard to keep going.'

'Yes, I can see that,' the counsellor acknowledges kindly.

'How often we just sing the words of songs in church, so familiar, such catchy tunes, get carried away with the music and don't really think about the words. I was reading about the background of the worship song "Blessed Be Your Name", written by Matt and Beth Redman. They quote a letter sent to them from a mother who had lost her eighteen-year-old daughter in a traffic accident.[56] I can relate so well to her words, speaking of how hard she found it to attend church afterwards, to worship again, to hear of all the good things that God has done, without having her daughter with her.'

The counsellor readjusts her scarf and sits back.

'The lyrics in that song are all about praising God in all circumstances, through the good times and the bad, when everything is going smoothly and when everything has fallen apart.

It makes me think about the child in the playground with the sweets who seemingly has a lot of friends. Will they still be hanging around when inevitably the sweets run out? Do the others like the child or like the sweets? It's the same with God when times are good and everything is going well: do we love him because of all the good things he provides or because of who he is?'

'I suppose it's in the hard times that you get to find out.'

I nod. 'Pete Greig, whom I've mentioned to you before in relation to prayer, talks about the bad times, about how important it is to admit them, to face them. He acknowledges that this can be difficult in church – that lots of worship songs can seem so upbeat, whatever the lyrics. He questions whether we are allowing space to express our deepest anguish within modern worship.'

'And what about you? Is this something that you feel?'

'Definitely. The world is full of sadness. It's a fallen world. It's not meant to be like this. There's sorrow and pain and it's a truth that can't be brushed away. Keller quotes some words from a book called *Spiritual Depression.* I haven't read that one! But the passage Keller quotes is all about facing grief, facing pain, facing suffering. And acknowledging it. It's about accepting that as Christians we will still feel despair and loss – we won't be immune to those feelings; that an absence of such feelings is

---

[56] *Blessed Be Your Name: Worshipping God on the Road Marked with Suffering;* Matt and Beth Redman.

unnatural; that as a Christian you will still experience them but, through faith, will be able to rise above them. It's a bit like I talked about before – Jesus helping us to plough through our grief despite us still feeling it.'

Somewhere down the corridor a door bangs. I can see outside that the wind is picking up. The counsellor shifts in her chair.

There's so much to say. I wonder how I'll fit everything into the session. But I carry on. 'I came across an article recently that sums up quite well the struggle the church can have with grief.[57] The writer too has lost a child. She makes the point that as the church is made up of people, it'll inevitably "mess up" and get things wrong, because people "mess up" and get things wrong. She emphasises that God loves his church and she loves the church, but in her grief, she's felt most comforted by non-Christian friends. Her conclusion is that the church needs to do better with grief. It needs to allow people to question, to cry, to feel let down, to be honest, in a non-judgemental, totally safe way where they can still feel loved, still feel accepted but with the space to do and be whatever is helpful. She acknowledges what I have mentioned to you before: that people can find it difficult to know how to help but sometimes the only way is simply by being there.'

'Is this article something that resonates with you?' the counsellor wants to know.

'Yes,' I say. 'The trouble is, it's a natural reaction to want to make things better. It's instinctive. Someone is upset so it's normal to try to comfort them, hush their crying, reassure them that things will improve. But the only way to the other side is by going through the middle. Grief can't be avoided or brushed aside. Soothing words that placate can "shut down" emotions. Sometimes you need the freedom to scream, the space to cry, for as long as you need.'

I look at the counsellor. She smiles and nods at me.

'But that's hard because it's against our basic instincts. It's like the parent who offers their child a plaster on their bumped knee because it's hurting; the child finds that taping up the knee doesn't stop the hurt after all and it may take longer to heal. We can't just paper over pain.'

'That's a good example,' the counsellor replies.

---

[57] *http://www.huffingtonpost.com/lexi-behrndt/making-room-for-grief-within-the-church-_b_7286748.html*

'A few months ago, we had a talk at church. The preacher mentioned a documentary about two families who'd both lost family members in the Hillsborough disaster. Apparently, one of the families had struggled with holding down jobs since the tragedy, whereas the other, which was Christian, had managed to keep their jobs going. The point of the speaker was that the Christian family had the hope of Jesus to sustain them in their grief and give them the strength to carry on. And whilst I completely agree that this hope is fundamental, it doesn't make you resistant to finding it difficult to slot back into everyday life. And this is OK. Talks like the one in church can be inspiring, but they can also add pressure. They can lead to feelings of inadequacy, feelings of not "measuring up". They can make it difficult to be honest about grief.'

'And what about you? Is this something that you have experienced?'

'Certainly. Another thing that I've found very hard is managing the difficulties other people have in knowing what to say to me. A conversation in which I volunteer information about Robbie becomes doubly hard, as simultaneously I am managing my own feelings and also managing those of the other person. And when I'm upset, a typical response can be, "Robbie wouldn't want to see you like this." What am I meant to do with that? It adds yet another layer: guilt that I've now also somehow let the side down; that I've let Robbie down; that I've disappointed him.'

There is a sympathetic nod from the counsellor.

'And I've found that a disclosure of the pain in our lives can often not get followed up or enquired about again, which, in a church full of people trying to be more Christ-like, I find bewildering. I want to tell people that it's OK to say that they don't understand. It's OK that they don't know what to say. But, for goodness' sake, please acknowledge it! Surely, grief hasn't made me invisible? Robbie's still my son and I want to talk about him just as I do my other children, just as they want to share with me about theirs.'

It's another area that I feel strongly about. I wouldn't be without Jesus by my side going through all this with me, but that doesn't change my circumstances. It doesn't bring Robbie back. The fact that Robbie is no longer physically here is the same if I'm a Christian or if I'm not a Christian.

'Like I said, church has been one of the hardest places for me to be and brings my loss into sharp focus. But shouldn't it be the place where

I find the most comfort, not just from the presence of God, as he's everywhere, but from the presence of those who are striving to be more like him, those with the most love to give?'

I think of the Bible verse for today that I read before I came out: 'Carry each other's burdens, and in this way you will fulfil the law of Christ.'[58]

'Until this happened,' I tell the counsellor, 'I didn't really think I'd many people to forgive. But now I have a long list. It's something that's really struck me: how many people have hurt me or have hurt the people I love.'

'Can you talk to me about it?' she asks.

It isn't easy to bring these memories back. I wonder whether the counsellor has any idea what she's asking, whether it's helpful to drag everything up. Is this what Jesus would want, this going over it all again?

> It is 2014. Wednesday, June 25th. I am in the back room and it is peaceful. The patio doors are open onto the garden, the roses in full bloom.
>
> The phone is ringing. It has become something to dread, an instrument of fear. Nigey answers. I can hear the murmur of his voice fading as he carries the phone down the hallway away from where I am sitting. But it isn't long before he is back. He has bad news.
>
> 'That was the coroner's office. It seems that the Defence have requested a second post-mortem.'
>
> There is a sudden piercing pain, a tightening of my stomach, a thudding in my ears. My heart will break all over again.
>
> 'They can't. They can't do that, surely? Not now. Not so late.'
>
> We have all been at least once. We have all seen Robbie. The post-mortem has been carried out, the results conclusive: an injury that could only have been caused by the impact of the crash. We have given clothes for Robbie to wear, put precious things with him. I am beyond words, incensed, furious, yet inside already defeated.
>
> Nigey is trying to explain to me that the Defence *can* do this. He has also spoken to Dick, the accident investigation officer. It

[58] Galatians 6:2.

is legal. But in over thirty years Dick has never heard of a post-mortem being requested after the body has been released for the funeral, except in murder cases. The only way to prevent it would be to refuse it – and then there would be no prosecution. It appears to be the way to get the car driver off the hook.

Gut-wrenching screams pour out of me. I am yelling and yelling and yelling; shrieking at the top of voice, making myself choke and gag and struggle to breathe, suffocating myself. Nigey is trying to get me to take a Valium tablet but I can't stop screaming and screaming and screaming. My boy, my poor son! Already in a handful of days his precious body has been taken to Frimley Park Hospital, Wrexham Park Hospital, the funeral place – and now he will have to go on to the Royal Berks Hospital for his body to be defiled again. I am livid. Fuming. *Where is the respect? Where is the remorse?*

'So there was another post-mortem. That must have been very hard.'

'It caused so much extra pain, so much trauma for me: the anguish of thinking of what they were doing coupled with the utter fury that they would request something so intrusive, seemingly to save their own skins. Of course, the investigation showed exactly what the previous one had. But, for me, it also introduced that doubt. I hadn't wanted to know the results of the first one but Kelly, our Family Liaison Officer, told me. The results were that the death was instant, and she knew that would help me. And so the request for the second one introduced a fear that the first result was wrong and that Robbie had maybe suffered a lot more.'

'That must have been so tough for you.'

'In the end, the request came in on the Wednesday and Robbie was transferred to the Royal Berks next day, but no one was available to perform the post-mortem until Monday. Tuesday was Robbie's service. We didn't even know until the day before if we were going to be able to go ahead with it. And all because of the Defence and the car driver.'

I try to pull my mind back to the present. I take out my phone and scroll down. 'This is from Matthew 6:12,' I say, reading out, '"Jesus said, 'And forgive us our debts, as we also have forgiven our debtors. And lead us not into temptation but deliver us from the evil one. For if you forgive other people when they sin against you, your heavenly Father will also forgive you. But if you do not forgive others their sins, your Father will not forgive your sins.'"[59] That's a powerful message, isn't it?' I note, looking up.

'Yes,' the counsellor agrees, waiting for me to go on.

'Remember the 50th wedding anniversary celebration for my parents at their church? I showed you the picture of Robbie helping his Granny down from the Land Rover.'

The counsellor smiles and nods. 'Yes, a lovely scene.'

'In their church is that stained glass window with Simon as a shepherd, the son of a previous vicar. During the trial of the man charged with the hit and run, of causing Simon's death, his dad, the vicar, asked for no punishment to be given to the man, reciting the Lord's prayer.' I think of Robbie. 'During the sentencing of the car driver, I prayed whilst the judge was deliberating – prayed that God would guide the judge; prayed that the sentence that God wanted would be the one given.' I pause, looking up into the counsellor's face. 'But the case was taken to court because I *did allow* that second post-mortem. I did want the car driver to face what had happened.'

I fall silent, thinking – thinking about all the mixed-up, confused emotions that I am trying to reconcile: how the image that I took away from court was of the car driver's parents sitting lost, alone, their son sent to prison; how I felt for them in their loss, but how I knew they would get their son back… God has certainly challenged me in the area of forgiveness.

'Recently I re-read sections of a book that I've haven't read for years. I probably haven't looked at it since I was in my twenties. It's by someone called Brother Ramon.[60] In the chapter on forgiveness, he says that when we repent, we receive God's gift of forgiveness, freely and undeservedly given. And we can use this gift to reach out and forgive those who've hurt us. But if we don't forgive them, this can cause a barrier, blocking God's forgiveness of us. So, in other words, we need to be able to forgive just as we've been forgiven, or it can be detrimental for our own forgiveness.'

'A two-way process,' the counsellor says, neatly summing up my clumsy sentence.

'That's right. Others put it in terms of a blackboard. Once God forgives us, the chalk is rubbed out and there's no record of our sin. And

[59] Matthew 6:12-15.
[60] *Forty Days and Forty Nights;* Brother Ramon SSF.

that's what's required of us when we forgive someone: a wiping out of past hurts; a blank page with no trace of what was once there.' I look down at the floor, at the swirly dark patches on the grey carpet tiles. 'Wow! I mean, how amazing to be able to do that! But how incredibly difficult! To remove that place from my mind which stores all those horrific, traumatizing events seems impossible.' *But,* I think to myself, *it's what Jesus has done for me.* Hanging on the cross, nailed under his hands was the full list of all my sins, past, present and future. The blood from his wounds flowed down causing the ink to run, so that there is now no record of them. Mind-blowing!

'The author of another book I dipped into recently believes that there are many layers to forgiveness – that we'll need to go through the forgiveness process again and again.[61] On one day, we feel able to forgive a particular wrong but on another we may seem unable to let it go. So forgiveness is a continual process, not just a one-off. By working through each layer, we get closer and closer to God.'

The counsellor nods.

I look up. 'So, I'm trying to forgive, but it isn't going to be an easy or quick journey.'

'No, of course not.'

'I try and pray for the car driver and the others who've hurt me and those I love, every day,' I say to the counsellor. 'I say to God that I choose to forgive them, that it's a conscious and deliberate action, and pray that their lives will be blessed by him.'

The counsellor is watching me, waiting as I search for the right words.

'Some days I know I'm simply saying the words – that there isn't much feeling behind them. And other days I know I'm trying to forgive because I know it's the right thing to do. But there are a few days when my heart is there too, when I find I do actually really mean it; I'm able to release them and release myself, and let the anger go. But it's a daily struggle, something I need to do over and over again.'

As the counsellor holds open the door, giving me an encouraging smile, I think again about Charlie Mackesy's painting of the cross. It'd make a good screensaver for my phone.

---

[61] Gerard W. Hughes; *Oh God, Why?*

I'm on the sofa relaxing when the photo is shown. A happy shot. A fun shot. The whole family crammed into the frame.

My heart is thumping. I'm holding my breath.

But there's no anticipation. No expectation.

Just a knowing. Just a knowing that he isn't there.

My face falls, my arms drop, my heart sinks. No Robbie then. No Robbie again.

Session 16

Revelation

'As soon as we got back from Cyprus, I needed to see him. I was desperate to see him. *Desperate.*'

The counsellor nods.

'We were back home from Cyprus early on Saturday morning. Everyone was at our house, and then Kelly and Dick (the accident investigation officer) came. People called round and on Sunday we went to church. I felt dazed, light-headed, disorientated. There was that tiny moment on waking when for a minute, a fraction, all was OK. And then I would remember – all over again.' I wipe my eyes, blow my nose. 'We couldn't see him until Monday. He had to be transferred from Frimley Park Hospital, where he was initially taken as the nearest place, to Wrexham Park for the post-mortem. Kelly took us in the police car twenty minutes down the M4. I used to go a lot to Wrexham Park, assessing babies born prematurely for work – so many of them amazing miracles of survival against the odds. And now, here I was, turning in to park by the mortuary to see my own son.'

'So, you were longing to see him but also finding it hard?'

'I was terrified too, yes. Kelly said that Robbie would be just as he was when he'd been brought in. She hadn't seen him and didn't know what kind of state that would mean. But someone had to identify him. We were in a small, narrow little room with some chairs and a door to the side where Robbie was. I was trembling, anxious, desperate to see him but hoping to discover that it wasn't him. I had no idea what to expect, how Robbie would be.'

Nigey goes through the door first with Kelly, while Dad is sitting beside me and holding my hand. I am crying.

In a matter of minutes, the door is opening and Nigey is here again.

'It's not Robbie. Tell me it's not Robbie. It can't be my Robbie.'

'It *is* Robbie. It's our Rob,' Nigey says. There is something about the way he is looking, something about how he sounds. He is calm, serene even, and there is something sanguine about his voice. 'Come. Come and see him.' He holds his hand out, then sensing my hesitation adds, 'It's OK. He looks OK. He looks just like Robs.'

He leads me in. And Robbie is here. My knees are weak and I feel my legs starting to buckle. *It's Robbie. My Robbie.* My whole body is shaking, shuddering. I am trying hard to control the sounds coming out of my mouth, trying not to shout. He is lying on a table, draped up to his neck in a white sheet. But I have seen him several times in hospital before in a similar way and this reassures me. His mouth is slightly open as though he is fast asleep. I reach out tentatively, but I don't touch his face. I know that he will feel cold and I can't deal with that. Instead I stoke his hair and kiss his head. His beard is doing well and he looks slightly unkempt, just as I have seen him look so many times before.

I am trembling, crying, totally overcome with every emotion. I am in this moment, *part of this moment* – me and my elder son. But it is only that: a moment. Soon we are being ushered out along with Tabby and Dad. Our slot is over. We have to move on. Other people are coming to see their loved one. The room is needed. This is the reality of life.

The tears fall unchecked down my cheeks, slip off my chin and splash onto my hand as I try to brush them away.

The counsellor gives me a moment. 'It must have been so moving for you,' she says.

'I had no idea leaving him then about how I would feel next time I saw him. I hadn't taken on board how painful and utterly real it would make things to see him in the coffin. I didn't cope then; I totally broke down, couldn't deal with it. But that first time… it's so odd but I wish I had a picture of Robbie, a photo of him "fast asleep" – so peaceful, so untroubled, so absolutely and completely at rest.'

The counsellor offers the tissue box and waits while I wipe my tears and dry my face.

'One of the Bible passages I find most comforting is in Thessalonians. I've read it so many times.' I find the verses on my phone and read them out. '"Brothers and sisters, we do not want you to be uninformed about those who sleep in death, so that you do not grieve like the rest of mankind, who have no hope. For we believe that Jesus died and rose again, and so we believe that God will bring with Jesus those who have fallen asleep in him."'[62]

'Yes, I can see why those words are so special to you.'

'It feels so soothing, "fallen asleep in him". One commentary I've come across says that the phrase-ology, terming death as having "fallen asleep" was used in the New Testament to refer to Christians who'd died.[63] There's three things it notes. One,' I say, 'just as when your body sleeps you continue to exist, so too does a Christian who's died. Two, when you sleep, your subconscious is still active in that you dream, so too for the Christian, the soul and spirit are still alive and awake in God's presence. Three, as sleep is only temporary, so too is the death of the body for the Christian, looking ahead to the resurrection.'

I think about this commentary that's in my 'favourites' on the PC at home. I would like to be able to share it with the counsellor, to let her see all the biblical passages that support this view. But there isn't enough time, and the PC is at home.

'That commentary gives me such hope,' I exclaim. 'I need that hope to keep going.'

The counsellor nods.

'Keller writes about hope. He says that without it, suffering can be unbearable. He points out that John wrote Revelation at a time when many Christians were suffering terrible persecution and unbelievable torture. However, they had the hope written about in Revelation of a "new heaven" and a "new earth" and unspeakable joys lying ahead. So when they were suffering, they sang hymns of praise and the more that people were killed, the more Christianity grew. Other people could see

---

[62] 1 Thessalonians 4:13-14.

[63] *https://bible.org/seriespage/comfort-his-coming-413-18*

that there was a difference with these Christian martyrs. They had a living hope. That's how they stayed strong.' I stop talking and think about how God has given *me* hope.

> It is evening on September 8th, 2015. I am on my way back from London. I have dropped Jack off at the Travelodge before the start of his cycle ride to Paris to raise funds in Robbie's memory. Now I am on my way home. It is getting late and is already dark. I am pleased his bike did fit in the car, relieved to have negotiated the journey here, and already tense not to have Jack beside me to guide me back. It was very hard leaving him. I am troubled about how he will stand up emotionally and physically to the three hundred miles ahead.
>
> I am nearly home, driving down the deserted A329(M) dual carriageway, passing the cemetery where Robbie's garden is and on a last stretch before turning off the main road. It is dark. There are no other vehicles around me, but suddenly I am aware of a black motorbike in the outside lane next to me that I haven't seen approach. I dip my headlights so that when it passes I won't dazzle it with my beam lights. But as I drive on, the motorbike doesn't pass me; and now, as I turn to see, it has completely disappeared. Vanished. But I know with absolute certainty a motorbike was there. My headlights are dipped ready. Was Robbie travelling alongside me? Or did God send an angel to accompany me in a form that I would recognise? As I drive home, my heart lifts. I know I'm not alone and that as I continue on this journey, walking with God through my pain and grief, I never will be.

'What a wonderful vision to hang on to.' The counsellor is looking at me, smiling.

'Oh yes! I was overjoyed – *am* still overjoyed – and feel so blessed that happened.' I think about how I got home and woke Nigey up, how I had to share it with him immediately, how I was overflowing with elation. 'Of course, though, I want that to happen again.'

'Naturally.'

'This chap Robert Weston has written about these sorts of experiences.[64] He says it's all about God moving back the veil between heaven and earth. He believes that God does this occasionally to give us comfort, but it isn't a general rule. He reminds us that we shouldn't go looking for chances to connect with people who've died, and that the scriptures forbid all types of divination.'

The counsellor nods.

'But I do notice signs that point to Robbie, whether it's a song in church that I know Robbie used to play, something someone says, a facial expression. And I'm always looking for rainbows. That first summer, I used to water the garden when the sun was out so that the light made rainbows in the water. They make me think of God's promises, God's faithfulness, and that picture of heaven in Revelation where a rainbow circles the throne.

'I was talking to the leaders of Upper Room where Robbie attended as a teenager – about heaven and my yearning to know what it's like. Then they told me the Dragonfly Story. I'd never heard it before.'

'The Dragonfly Story? I don't know that one. What happens?'

'Well, it's a wonderful way to portray the problem of describing heaven. How, for example, do you describe green or any other colour to someone who has no sight? In a recent sermon at church we were told that if someone who has been born blind has their sight restored, it can take up to two years to comprehend the things that they can now visualise. We often say, "Oh yes, I see now," meaning, "Oh yes, I *understand* now." There are no words or understanding in the human world for a vision of heaven.'

'So how does the story go?'

'In the muddy, murky water below the lily pads, there lived a community of water beetles,' I begin, hoping I can remember the lovely story accurately and do it justice. 'All day they moved about down there in their own little world, knowing nothing different. But once in a while, sadness would come upon them as a beetle climbed the stem of a lily and disappeared and they knew they would never see them again. One day, one little beetle felt an irresistible urge to climb the lily stem. He told his friend that he wouldn't disappear as the others had but he would come

---

[64] *Experiencing Growth Through Loss;* Robert Weston. *www.ruachministries.org/valeoftears/p8fresistingmakingcontact.htm*

back and tell him what was up there. So up he went and at the top climbed out of the pond. After he'd emerged from the other side, his body began to change and suddenly he was no longer a water beetle but a dragonfly. The world he was now in was so stunning, so beautiful. He didn't know how he was ever going to find the words to describe it to his friend who only knew the murkiness of the world on the other side at the bottom of the pond, but he'd tell his friend as he promised him he would. But when he tried to go back under the water, he couldn't. He couldn't return to that former world now he had wings and had been transformed for other things. So, the dragonfly is physically transformed; just like we'll be.'

'That's charming.'

'Yes, it's a really useful little story. But quite powerful. Pete Greig says that after his resurrection, Jesus was still recognisable as a person but not instantly recognisable as Jesus. His body still had the marks from the crucifixion but can't have looked startlingly unusual as no one seems to have given the risen Jesus a second look; the disciples on the road to Emmaus just thought they were talking to an ordinary person. His resurrected body allowed him to walk through walls but also eat real food. He could still have relationships with people and express emotion. So Greig concludes that maybe our resurrected bodies, though different, will be surprisingly normal.'

I think about that angel costume that Robbie wore for the Year 6 nativity. I think about how simplistic our human minds are – how naïve to believe that a strand of tinsel and strip of white cloth will suffice.

'In that Lent book we studied in church, Graham Tomlin explains the resurrection of the body by looking at the natural world. A bulb, after flowering, withers, dies and starts to decay. There's no evidence of its continued existence under the ground. Yet the following spring, a new shoot appears and the flower emerges again. The resulting plant looks nothing like the bulb in the soil. But the bulb continues to exist. It isn't replaced by the shoots and flower; rather, the plant emerges as part of the original bulb. Tomlin suggests that in this way, the resurrected body will be continuous with the old self.

'It reminds me of that poem Robbie's pupils wrote about the raindrop. And this passage,' I say, fishing my phone out again. 'Well, actually two passages: 1 Corinthians 15:36-37 and 42-44. "What you sow does not come to life unless it dies. When you sow, you do not plant the body that will be, but just a seed, perhaps of wheat or of something else," and, "The body that is sown is perishable, it is raised imperishable; it is sown in dishonour, it is raised in glory; it is sown in weakness, it is raised in power; it is sown a natural body, it is raised a spiritual body."'

I look up at the counsellor, then reach up to my necklace and hold Robbie's thumbprint tightly in my hand.

'The Evangelist Billy Graham,' I say, 'wrote that he was often asked by people whether they will recognise and be reunited with those they have loved when they die.[65] And he replied that the answer is a definite yes.' I am aware that I am smiling; a huge grin is breaking out, spreading across my face. 'Sheldon adds that from all the accounts he has examined of near death and time of death experiences, every person that is sighted is someone who was known to the dying person.'

I look up and meet the counsellor's eyes. They are shining, beaming back at me.

'Revelation 22:1-5,' I read out to her. '"Then the angel showed me the river of the water of life, as clear as crystal, flowing from the throne of God and of the Lamb down the middle of the great street of the city. On each side of the river stood the tree of life, bearing twelve crops of fruit, yielding its fruit every month. And the leaves of the tree are for the healing of the nations. No longer will there be any curse. The throne of God and of the Lamb will be in the city, and his servants will serve him. They will see his face, and his name will be on their foreheads. There will be no more night. They will not need the light of a lamp or the light of the sun, for the Lord God will give them light. And they will reign for ever and ever."'

Suddenly time is up.

---

[65] *The Heaven Answer Book;* Billy Graham

It is early morning. Very early. The sun is just starting to creep round the edges of the curtains. And there are birds awake. The sounds filter through to me as I drift in and out of sleep. I am at home, in the kitchen, when I hear a new noise: the sound of keys and the front door being opened. Then Robbie's voice calling out hello.

I rush through to the hall and he is there, standing on the mat, smiling. I collapse onto him and hold him tightly, breathing in the smell of him, and grasping the solid firmness of his frame, his physical being.

And I'm sobbing, 'I love you. I love you, Robbie.'

'Love you too, Mum,' he grins at me. But he is pulling away, getting ready to leave. 'I can't stay Mum; I've got to go and see someone who has Barrett's oesophagus and has just had bad news. I was allowed to come here as you've been so upset but that doesn't usually happen.'

Then I watch as he walks down the drive and simply disappears. But I awake with such joy and hope – *I have seen him again.*

References / Bibliography

Books

Walking with God Through Pain and Suffering, Timothy Keller, Hodder and Stoughton (2013)

Finding God in the Shack, Randal Rauser, Biblica Publishing (2009)

Paradoxology, Krish Kandiah, Hodder and Stoughton (2014)

When Bad Things Happen to Good People, Harold S. Kushner, PAN Books (1992)

The Shack, William Young, Hodder (2007)

Hidden Christmas, Timothy Keller, Hodder and Stoughton (2016)

Blind Spots in the Bible, Adrian Plass, The Bible Reading Fellowship (2006)

50 Things you Need to Know About Heaven, Dr John Hart, Bethany House, Baker Publishing Group (2014)

Near Death: A Biblical Journey, Eli H. Sheldon, CrossBooks (2011)

Perspective, Sir Henry Scott Holland

Blessed Be Your Name: Worshipping God on the Road Marked With Suffering, Matt and Beth Redman, Hodder and Stoughton (2005)

God on Mute, Pete Greig, Kingsway Communications Ltd (2007)

Forty Days and Forty Nights, Brother Ramon SSF, Marshall Pickering (1993)

What's in a Word, David Winter, The Bible Reading Fellowship (1994)

Oh God, Why? Gerard W Hughes, The Bible Reading Fellowship (1993)

Marking Time, Nick Baines, St Andrew's Press (2005)

The Dragonfly Story, Anon.

Looking through the Cross, Graham Tomlin, Bloomsbury (2013)

The Heaven Answer Book, Billy Graham, Thomas Nelson (2012)

Journals / Newspapers

ITV Meridan 13th June, 2014

http://www.itv.com/news/meridian/story/2014-06-13/fatal-collision-in-finchampstead/

'Have the British Forgotten How to Grieve?' Clover Stroud

http://www.telegraph.co.uk/news/health/10639359/Have-the-British-forgotten-how-to-grieve.html

'Taboo and the different death? Perceptions of those bereaved by suicide or other traumatic death.' Chapple, Ziebland, Hawton, *Sociology of Health and Illness* (2015)

http://www.ncbi.nlm.nih.gov/pubmed/25683372

Tribute by Vineyard Church

http://www.getreading.co.uk/news/local-news/talented-popular-science-teacher-greatly-7287594

'Making Room for Grief Within the Church', Lexi Behrndt

http://www.huffingtonpost.com/lexi-behrndt/making-room-for-grief-within-the-church-_b_7286748.html (accessed 27.5.16)

Websites

'Messages for Unique Funeral Situations (5) "God's Time" in the face of what seemed an untimely death'

https://bible.org/series/messages-unique-funeral-situations (accessed 3.1.16)

Why did God harden Pharaoh's heart?

http://christiananswers.net/q-aiia/aiia-pharaoh.html

How does God harden the heart?

http://fryroad.org/_fryroad/BibleStudy/Salvation/HowDoesGodHardentheHeart/tabid/172/Default.aspx

'Does God still work miracles today?' Jack Wellman

http://www.whatchristianswanttoknow.com/does-god-still-work-miracles-today/

Farnborough Hill School

http://www.cisc.uk.net/index.php/home/news/115-farnborough-hill-teacher-dies-in-tragic-accident

Quote from Mother Teresa

https://www.goodreads.com/quotes/664276-it-is-not-how-much-we-do-but-how-much

Robbie Schofield tribute page

https://www.facebook.com/robbieschofield.1987

Matthew Henry Commentary on John 19

http://www.jesus.org/death-and-resurrection/last-words/why-did-jesus-say-woman-behold-your-son.html

The National Association for Christian Recovery – 'Forgiving as Prayer', Juanita Ryan

http://www.nacr.org/wordpress/3699/forgiving-as-prayer

'The comfort of his coming – 1 Thessalonians 4'

https://bible.org/seriespage/comfort-his-coming-413-18

'Experiencing Growth Through Loss', Robert Weston

http://www.ruachministries.org/valeoftears/p8fresistingmakingcontact.htm

Jesus raises Lazarus

https://www.biblegateway.com/resources/commentaries/IVP-NT/John/Jesus-Raises-Lazarus

Complications of Meckel diverticulum

http://www.msdmanuals.com/home/children-s-health-issues/digestive-disorders-in-children/meckel-diverticulum

Abdominal adhesions

http://www.2minutemedicine.com/patient-basics-abdominal-adhesions/

http://www.londongeneralsurgeryclinic.co.uk/abdominal-adhesions.php

Barrett's oesophagus

http://patient.info/health/barretts-oesophagus-leaflet

What Shall I Read Next?

A Valley Journal
Abi May
ISBN 978-1-907509-99-5

There is little in life that prepares us for the loss of those people most dear to us, whether through a prolonged decline in health or terminal illness, or the shock and trauma experienced through sudden or accidental death.

This book has been written to help those who are grieving to explore the memories, emotions and thoughts around their bereavement ex-perience, and at different stages of the bereavement journey.

Abi May speaks from her own heart and experiences to help guide others through their individual journeys, and her depth of understanding and compassion speaks volumes as the pages are turned.

Losing Tom, Finding Grace
Jackie Slough
ISBN 978-1-907509-07-0

Written as a journal it is an honest and intimate revelation of one woman's ability to cope with the unexpected suicide of her teenage son.

Tom was a deep-thinking and creative young man, and an active Christian. How can a young Christian commit suicide? How can a parent not feel condemned? What goes through the minds of people in these circumstances? Excerpts from Tom's diary are included.

You will find it difficult to put this book down. As you read through the emotional honesty of this narrative, you will wonder at God's amazing grace.

Books available from all good bookshops,
or directly from the publisher:

www.onwardsandupwards.org